D1055043

# THE RIGHTS OF GOD

Advancing Human Rights
Sumner B. Twiss, John Kelsay, Terry Coonan, Series Editors

**Editorial Board**

Nigel Biggar
Stanley Cohen
Michael Davis
Mark Ensalaco
Gerrie ter Haar
Rhoda E. Howard-Hassmann
Simeon Ilesanmi
John Langan, SJ
David Little
Dan Maier-Katkin
Juan E. Mendez
Ann Elizabeth Moore
Michael H. Posner
Fernando Teson

*Agenda Setting, the UN, and NGOs: Gender Violence and Reproductive Rights*
Jutta M. Joachim

*Breaking Silence: The Case That Changed the Face of Human Rights*
Richard Alan White

*For All Peoples and All Nations: The Ecumenical Church and Human Rights*
John S. Nurser

*Freedom from Want: The Human Right to Adequate Food*
George Kent

*Power and Principle: Human Rights Programming in International Organizations*
Joel E. Oestreich

*Protecting Human Rights: A Comparative Study*
Todd Landman

*The Rights of God: Islam, Human Rights, and Comparative Ethics*
Irene Oh

# THE RIGHTS OF GOD

## *Islam, Human Rights, and Comparative Ethics*

IRENE OH

Georgetown University Press / Washington, D.C.

Clinton College Library

As of January 1, 2007, 13-digit ISBN numbers have replaced the 10-digit system.

| 13-digit | | 10-digit | |
|---|---|---|---|
| Paperback: | 978-1-58901-184-7 | Paperback: | 1-58901-184-8 |
| Cloth: | 978-1-58901-185-4 | Cloth: | 1-58901-185-6 |

Georgetown University Press, Washington, D.C. www.press.georgetown.edu
© 2007 by Georgetown University Press. All rights reserved. No part of this book may be reproduced or utilized in any form or by any means, electronic or mechanical, including photocopying and recording, or by any information storage and retrieval system, without permission in writing from the publisher.

Library of Congress Cataloging-in-Publication Data
Oh, Irene.
The rights of God : Islam, human rights, and comparative ethics / Irene Oh.
p. cm. — (Advancing human rights)
Includes bibliographical references and index.
ISBN 978-1-58901-185-4 (hardcover : alk. paper)—ISBN 978-1-58901-184-7 (pbk. : alk. paper)
1. Islam and civil society. 2. Human rights—Religious aspects—Islam. 3. Islam and humanism. I. Title.
BP173.63.O3 2007
297.2'72—dc22
2007007016

♾ This book is printed on acid-free paper meeting the requirements of the American National Standard for Permanence in Paper for Printed Library Materials.

14 13 12 11 10 09 08 07     9 8 7 6 5 4 3 2
First printing

Printed in the United States of America

# CONTENTS

# ACKNOWLEDGMENTS

A book about conversation and dialogue would not have been possible without many conversations and dialogues. *The Rights of God* was conceived while I was a graduate student at the University of Virginia, where I had the good fortune of conversing with a number of inspiring scholars and teachers. I thank James Childress, Charles Mathewes, Ann Monius, Aziz Sachedina, and Michael J. Smith especially for their time and commitment. I must also express my gratitude to John Kelsay, who has been a generous and insightful mentor, and to Sohail Hashmi for his guidance and humanity. Liz Bucar, Tal Lewis, Grace Kao, Jonathan Schofer, and Aaron Stalnaker have offered their friendship, knowledge, and support. The Center on Religion and Democracy provided me a year to research and write, as well as an environment that stimulated lively conversations with a wonderful group of young scholars. Notre Dame's Erasmus Institute also enabled me to work on this manuscript while the work was still in its infancy. Jens Böel at the UNESCO archives in Paris provided valuable assistance in researching early dialogues about human rights. The Irmgard Coninx Foundation and Humboldt Universität provided a forum for discussing shared interests with an international group of human rights scholars and activists. I also thank Dexter Callender, John Fitzgerald, David Graf, Henry Green, David Kling, Michelle Gonzalez Maldonado, Ada Orlando, Ivan Petrella, Jenni Ratner-Rosenhagen, and Stephen Sapp, all at the University of Miami, for their true collegiality. Finally, I am thankful for the daily conversations I have with my husband, James. In acknowledging him for his constant support, I am reminded that there are occasions in life when words are inadequate to express the depths of gratitude.

# INTRODUCTION

Promoting Islam as a defender of human rights is fraught with difficulties. Many advocates of human rights readily point out the numerous examples of humanitarian failures carried out in the name of Islam: the Taliban in Afghanistan, female genital mutilation in Africa, the penal code in Saudi Arabia, genocide in Darfur, and the September 11 attacks in the United States. As a result, human rights proponents are often tempted to blame Islam, if not religion generally, for human rights violations. The avoidance of Islam and religion in human rights dialogue presents a serious problem for the advancement of universal human rights, however.

Separating religious belief from human rights requires that we undertake the impossible task of distinguishing an important source of our ethical values from ethical norms themselves. For many people, the validity of human rights stems from a foundational belief in God and the dignity that God imparts to every human being. Although the foundations of human rights may be debated, human rights scholars cannot easily dismiss the potential that foundational beliefs, including Islam, hold in advancing human rights agendas. After all, approximately one billion inhabitants of this earth identify themselves as Muslim. To ignore the values of Islam would be to deny the voices of one-fifth of the world's population in determining what should be "universal" human rights.

Unfortunately, human rights theorists are frequently at odds when attempting to engage in discourse with religious thinkers. This discomfort with discussing religion arises not only as a result of religiously motivated violations of human rights but also because of structural differences among the modes of discourse relevant to human rights. These differences include the disciplinary dominance of human rights as legal or political discourse, Western liberal paradigms that assert the privatization of foundational belief, and the interdisciplinary boundaries between religion and human rights theory. Thomas Pogge observes, for example, that the shift away from religion to politics as the appropriate sphere for human rights discourse can be attributed to the shift in conceptions of morality based in natural law and duties to that of rights.[1] Using the religious language of natural law and duties in human rights discussions appears antiquated and inappropriate in this day and age. John Rawls, although acknowledging that persons belonging to pluralistic societies often subscribe to foundational beliefs, asserts nonetheless that in public discourse on political values, religious language should be limited to that which "reasonable" persons may endorse.[2] Persons who use religious ideas in public debates on human rights may seem unreasonable to those who do not share those beliefs. Michael Ignatieff argues that the prima facie human capacity to empathize serves as a much better basis for human rights compared to the capricious nature of religious traditions. Such theoretical tensions hinder what should be fruitful exchanges between human rights theorists and religious thinkers.[3]

## COMPARATIVE RELIGIOUS ETHICS

I propose comparative religious ethics as a method for bringing religious thought into the fold of human rights theory. A relatively new field in the academic study of religion, comparative religious ethics seeks to understand ethical values across religions and cultures. A comparative effort here is particularly fruitful because "Western" human rights theorists from North America and Western Europe struggle to understand the human rights violations found in "non-Western" Islamic societies of the Middle East and Southeast Asia.[4] Comparative religious ethics provides a methodological structure for difficult but necessary interreligious and cross-cultural conversations about human rights and Islam.

Admittedly, the "pleasant trope of 'conversation'" that often accompanies a comparative enterprise can appear oddly misplaced, given the harsh reality of human cruelty and suffering that characterizes much of human rights study. Conversation and "dialogue," the latter of which, despite its more serious connotation, is used interchangeably with the former, are nonetheless necessary if one attempts to undertake the task of understanding another person, culture, or tradition.[5]

As Charles Taylor asserts, any "adequate account of human action must make the agents more understandable." The dialogical model aids with understanding persons from different traditions and cultures than one's own because it recognizes those persons as agents like oneself, "i.e., beings who act, have purposes, desires."[6] To understand others as agents requires that we view them as possessing self-understanding rather than unilaterally categorize them as mere objects of study. In acknowledging others as self-understanding humans, we need not necessarily agree with them, but we avoid the danger of objectifying them and preventing genuine dialogue from taking place. We allow, if not expect, self-representation of all participants, which is essential for any meaningful conversation to develop. In dialogue that promotes understanding, others have voices, and we are required over the course of conversation to acknowledge and respond to those voices. Moreover, and just as important, we recognize through such dialogue our own assumptions, the limits of our knowledge, and the possibilities for understanding, and we therefore present human faces to our interlocutors.

Because this reciprocative model of dialogue requires self-understanding, we must account for the political and historical conditions that influence our own perceptions.[7] In the postcolonial context, which characterizes many Muslim societies, both the memory and the present reality of unequal power relations taint conversations between persons who, if only symbolically, represent the colonized and the colonizer. In the specific case of dialogue between Islamic thinkers from previously colonized societies and North American and European thinkers, the colonial experience exists as a subtext of human rights discourse. Although the colonial experience is prominent in writings on human rights by Islamic scholars, it is not explicitly acknowledged on the part of human rights theorists. The dialogical aspect of comparative religious ethics requires that this background be brought into the foreground so that we better understand the agents of human rights discourse. If Islamic thinkers from previously colonized societies enter into a dialogue about human rights with the self-understanding of persons who were previously colonized, then this experience suggests to Western human rights theorists, as interlocutors, that they, too, consider colonialism in understanding Islam and human rights.

Allowing others to define themselves, however, does not require that we adopt their perspectives as our own. Even if it were possible, one need not let go of one's own perspective in order to understand another. Understanding is not an either-or proposition that requires the adoption of polarities. One need neither lose the ability to critique another perspective nor fall into the abyss of moral relativism by entering into a conversation reflective of all possible views. Rather, through the process of dialogue, interlocutors come to understand better a shared subject matter.

Heavily indebted to Hans-Georg Gadamer's conception of the "fusion of horizons," my approach to comparative religious ethics incorporates a dialogical model of understanding to contemporary Islamic thought and human rights theory. Gadamer argues that dialogue based on a shared subject matter, in this case human rights, leads participants in conversation toward a shared vision even while standing in separate places. The major adaptation I make to Gadamer's conception of fusion of horizons is to incorporate Jürgen Habermas's sensitivity to the distortion of language. Given that my work in comparative ethics deals with Islam and human rights, a field in which perceptions of political and economic inequalities are intrinsic to discussion, Habermas's insights heighten awareness of obstacles in the way of cross-cultural understanding.

In approaching Islamic human rights with this dialogical model of understanding, I both build on and depart from earlier works in comparative religious ethics. Because the idea of human rights finds acceptability across the globe, I begin this comparative project with an issue that has universal significance. Notable in this respect is that a spectrum of Islamic scholars embraces the concept of human rights, even as differences arise with regard to specific claims about human rights. My undertaking of a comparative project with a universal idea such as human rights shares some common ground with the path-breaking work of David Little and Sumner B. Twiss.[8] Little and Twiss, who seek a universal account of moral concepts through empirical case studies, commence with the possibility of universal bases for comparison. Although they do not use human rights as one of their moral concepts, human rights would fit within the structure of their study. I differ from Little and Twiss as to the process by which moral concepts are defined, however. Little and Twiss themselves offer definitions of specific moral concepts as starting points for discussion. By contrast, universal human rights should be theoretically defined, or at least agreed on, by a collective group of persons representing different nations, traditions, and cultures. In my study, I do not define human rights as a moral concept but rather question whether the static identification of human rights with lists of specific rights, such as those found in the Universal Declaration of Human Rights (UDHR, adopted by the United Nations in 1948), makes sense given the cultural, historical, and religious diversity of the societies in which these rights are to be respected and implemented.

My examination of human rights borrows much from Lee Yearley's work in comparative ethics, which compares the virtue of courage in the writings of Mencius and Aquinas. Yearley's observation that ideas share genuine resemblances across cultures offers much for human rights discussions. As he eloquently states, comparative religious ethics charts "similarities within differences and differences within similarities."[9] Yearley, although he narrows the scope of comparative ethics by examining one specific aspect of human flourishing, moves beyond Little and Twiss in allowing for the modification of terms and their meanings based on analogies uncovered through the comparative process. This openness to modification applies to the understanding of human rights as a concept still subject to interpretation. Of equal import, Yearley views the effort of comparison itself as a moral exercise of increasing significance in our diverse world. Not a mere intellectual endeavor, the practice of comparative religious ethics carries profound moral implications for the times in which we live.

Similar to the dialogical method proposed by Gadamer and Taylor, Yearley's approach to comparative ethics requires movement between at least two interlocutors about a shared subject matter. Conscious of becoming too self-referential, participants in this dialogical process would find this approach especially appropriate for a subject matter of universal significance, such as human rights. Discussed globally with shared urgency, the topic of human rights brings to comparative religious ethics "a more persuasive rationale, agenda of ideas, and practical orientation than hitherto has been the case."[10] Comparative religious ethics brings to human rights the tools and methods necessary for understanding religions in a pluralistic and troubled world.

## UNDERSTANDING ISLAM

I am a scholar trained in religious ethics, initially in Western philosophical and Christian ethics and later in Islamic ethics, and am deeply concerned with a tradition that is not my own. Islam is important and relevant to me as a scholar, teacher, and citizen, but I am not a Muslim. Using human rights as the subject of cross-cultural inquiry, I believe that a core set of shared values exists universally and that the values peripheral to these basic rights must be respected in light of religious and cultural diversity. One of my objectives is to demonstrate that very human concerns cross religious and cultural boundaries.

The more one learns about a religious tradition, and the differences within the larger tradition, the more one understands that arguments for relative values can become almost a matter of course. Acknowledging these differences and observing particularities, as Clifford Geertz explains, are essential to understanding a subject.[11] In his call for "thick description," we are rightly forced not to objectify and stereotype and simplify the other. Instead, we see in the uniqueness of people, acts, and situations the complexity of humans and history.

The call to particularity, although it corrects many of the inaccurate assumptions that scholars may make about religious belief and practice, obscures the prima facie observation that, for all our differences, we are in many ways alike. On the most basic, biological level, we all require food, water, shelter, and other humans to survive from infancy to adulthood. Humans tend to live in social groups, engage in commerce, and adopt cultural rituals. Moreover, we value many of the same things. Although exceptions always exist, people value freedom, peace, and health and find torture, terror, and tyranny wrong. Humans are capable of engaging with each other across cultures not because we are so different from one another but because we are so similar.

## THREE THINKERS, THREE VISIONS

In the decades preceding and following the creation of the UDHR, Islamic religious scholars offered numerous commentaries on the concept of human rights that was slowly but surely entering into the world milieu. They wrote about human rights from numerous angles, often in praise, but also in highly critical and sometimes angry tones. Their ideas are important because of the tremendous influence they exerted, and continue to exert, among Muslims at large.

The value of religious scholarship, particularly in examining human rights issues of the contemporary Islamic world, cannot be overemphasized. For guidance on religious and political issues, Muslims have tended to look toward religious authorities rather than political leaders, who have acquired reputations either as puppets of foreign interests or as weak, ineffectual, and ultimately insignificant figureheads. Muslims have taken far more seriously the thoughts of religious leaders, whose commentaries were heard or read or were otherwise transmitted by local clerics. Political documents, such as the 1981 Universal Islamic Declaration of Human Rights (UIDHR), although certainly important in understanding human rights in Islamic thought, reveal but part of a much larger story.

The thinkers whose writings I analyze here provide the substance for dialogue on human rights. The topics they address and the methods they use to think about these topics can and should be used in conversations about religious diversity. Most important, these scholars offer ways of addressing social injustice that are alternatives to acts of violence. For instance, although Islamic scholars such as Abul A'la Maududi and Sayyid Qutb have been cited as the inspiration behind acts of religious violence, their writings leave much to interpretation.[12] Indeed, on close analysis the essence of their messages concerns the empowerment of Muslims in colonial and postcolonial contexts, not the destruction of non-Muslims.

This book shows how three of the most prominent religious scholars writing about human rights can contribute to a global understanding of human rights. The scholars I have selected to focus on are Maududi, Qutb, and 'Abdolkarim Soroush, each of whom offers a distinct approach to Islam and human rights. They offer a representative range of views that challenge not only assumptions about the role of religion in human rights but also the idea of a monolithic Islam. Writing at a time when the concept of human rights unfolds across the international landscape, these thinkers demonstrate a perspicacious grasp of the potential significance of human rights. They sense that the novel, but extraordinarily powerful, language of human rights must somehow be molded into Islamic thought.

Although many scholars of Islam have written about human rights, Maududi, Qutb, and Soroush stand out for several reasons. First, Maududi and Qutb are scholars whose influence cannot be underestimated in Muslim-majority countries. Soroush, although not as well known in part because he is of a younger generation than Maududi and Qutb, has gained increasing prominence for both his intellectual and political roles in Iran and the larger Shi'ite community. Well-known American scholars, such as Abdullahi An-Na'im and Ann Mayer, have written extensively on human rights, but their influence is felt primarily in North American and Western European audiences.[13] Because this book examines human rights from a cross-cultural perspective, specifically at the ways in which non-Western Islamic thinkers perceive of human rights, understanding the voices of scholars outside of North America or Western Europe is of utmost importance. Moreover, the influence of Maududi, Qutb, and Soroush within Muslim-majority societies suggests that their opinions on human rights carry more weight than those of scholars who are not as well known in those settings.

Second, Maududi, Qutb, and Soroush have produced significant works on human rights. Other prominent Islamic scholars have produced numerous essays and shorter pieces on human rights and related topics, but Maududi, Qutb, and Soroush are notable for their extensive and sustained writing on the subject.[14] They explore multiple facets of human rights, their theological underpinnings and implications, and the differences between Western and Islamic views of human rights. Few major works from influential Islamic thinkers in Muslim-majority societies delve into such depth about human rights.

The writings I focus on in this book treat the topic of human rights at length. Maududi's *Human Rights in Islam,* Qutb's *Social Justice in Islam,* and Soroush's collected works in the aptly titled *Reason, Freedom, and Democracy in Islam* address directly the topic of human rights (*huquq al insaniyya*) as well as the many issues that relate to the subject indirectly. The three thinkers offer collectively a prolific number of published texts, many of which reinforce their ideas found in their writings dealing specifically with human rights. Qutb, for instance, echoes and elaborates on several of his ideas from *Social Justice in Islam* in his lengthy Qur'anic commentary, *In the Shade of the Qur'an*.[15] Their most relevant thoughts on human rights, however, are found in their treatises that concentrate on the topics of justice, politics, and religion. The main human rights texts from the three authors were also written after the drafting of the UDHR, which introduced the idea of human rights to the world in an official capacity. Although the language of human rights existed prior to 1948, the formal introduction of human rights through the United Nations, an internationally acknowledged institution, lent the term a gravity and context that previously did not exist. Hence, writings published after 1948 treat human rights with an awareness and sensitivity to this new setting that writings published before 1948 lack.

Maududi's and Qutb's book-length treatments of human rights express forcefully their views on how Islam promotes human rights. Moreover, they clearly situate their analyses within the context of the twentieth century and bring religious understanding to bear on modern times and modern problems. Also, these texts directly compare Islamic views on human rights to Western ones. Soroush's collection of essays, written several decades after Maududi's and Qutb's works, continues an intra-Islamic discussion on human rights. Like Maududi's and Qutb's writings, Soroush's essays display an awareness of the author's own historical context and also demonstrate how religious tradition applies to contemporary issues. Soroush brings Western thought into his writings on Islam, albeit with a very different attitude compared to Maududi and Qutb. All three authors highlight in their comprehensive scholarship similar aspects of human rights, namely, democracy, toleration, and freedom of conscience. Because these major works on human rights share structural and thematic similarities but offer different analyses within those similarities, they are ideal for initiating a conversation on human rights.

Third, and important to the practice of cross-cultural and interreligious dialogue, these thinkers' writings on human rights have attained a stature such that they are available in translation. The high quality of these translations, predominantly from Arabic into English, allows for more profound conversations on human rights because interlocutors who may not know Arabic are able to read for themselves what Islamic scholars have to offer to human rights discussions. I relied primarily on English translations of these writings on human rights, although I referred to the original Arabic texts when I wanted to ensure the accuracy of a certain translation or sought to determine nuances of specific theological or political terms.[16] In those instances when I referred back to the original, I did not find the translated version to be so inaccurate as to mislead the English reader.

A fourth reason why I chose to focus on Maududi, Qutb, and Soroush was to cover the breadth of Islamic thought typically categorized as "fundamentalist" or "traditionalist" on the one hand and "reformist," "liberal," or "intellectual" on the other. These labels are often applied to Islamic thinkers as a cursory description of their attitudes toward the West and modernization. Fundamentalist or traditionalist thinkers, such as Maududi and Qutb, appear to be intolerant of the West and seem wary of modernization. Liberal or reformist intellectuals, such as Soroush, appear to embrace the West and view modernization as a positive trend. These descriptions, although they provide an initial orientation to a scholar's thought, are not adequate to convey the complexities involved in each thinker's arguments. These labels also betray the history within Islamic thought of reforms based in traditional texts and legal theory. Thus, although the terms "traditionalist" and "reform" appear to sit at opposite ends of the ideological spectrum, the terms can only be understood so at the most superficial level. This categorization of ideologies as ranging from traditionalist to reform thus provides a bereft, albeit convenient, overview of the Islamic scholars' ideas.

Finally, the differences in geographical and historical contexts among the three thinkers make impossible the portrayal of Islam as a monolithic tradition. Distinct colonial experiences color Maududi's, Qutb's, and Soroush's ways of thinking about Islam and its applicability in political settings. Maududi, for example, shares with Qutb many similar views of Islam; however, the situation of the Muslim minority in India and the creation of the state of Pakistan result in the liberalizing of certain aspects of Maududi's thought, especially toward non-Muslims and women. When placed in historical contexts, these scholars' different views of Islam become clearer.

To understand these nuances of Islamic thought, one needs to examine how religious scholars make their arguments. Only through such analyses can one grasp fully the coherence and inconsistencies of religious arguments. An overview of many thinkers may provide a bird's-eye view of the landscape of contemporary Islamic thought, but it denies close examination of the texture of their arguments. From a practical perspective, deep analyses convey accurate depictions of their ideas, as opposed to noncontextual glosses that enable the exploitation of genuine religious scholarship for unjustifiable, even violent, purposes. Crucial to the task of cross-cultural conversation, providing a sustained discussion about these three men and their thoughts gives cross-cultural debate a human face. Without constant reminders, we are prone to forget that our conversation partners are, as Taylor reminds us, agents of self-understanding. For these reasons, I have chosen to concentrate on three thinkers whose scholarship best represents variations in Islamic thought on human rights.

## DIALOGUE AND HUMAN RIGHTS

On one level, this book tells the story of how three revered scholars from three different countries grapple intellectually with the notion of human rights. These scholars interpret not only religious text and scripture but also the political events surrounding them. The differences among the thinkers represent the ways in which religion works through changing historical, geographical, and intellectual contexts. The variances in setting, culture, and background of these thinkers emerge in their writings. When the concept of human rights developed into a global idea, Islamic thinkers embraced it primarily because they embraced the religious principles they saw in it. The commentaries they provided on the topic of human rights reveal their ways of incorporating human rights into religious worldviews.

On another level, and of most importance, this book offers ways of engaging critically with others about human rights and Islam. Some of the most prominent theories of human rights in the West today dismiss Islam altogether with claims that religion generally presents obstacles to human rights progress.[17] In analyzing the commentaries of Islamic thinkers, however, we can perceive distinctions between *religious* arguments concerning human rights and *political* ones regarding the struggle for power. The most disturbing claims about human rights made by Islamic scholars result not from religious ideals but from strategies developed out of an intense fear and hatred of Western colonialists. Those who dismiss religious contributions to human rights fail to separate religious arguments from political and cultural tactics intended to undo the perceived damages wrought by imperialism. This is not to say that disentangling politics and culture from religion is an easy, or even possible, task; however, the attempt must be undertaken in order to understand and overcome the crippling history of colonialism that prevents genuine dialogue from taking place across religious and cultural boundaries. The living memory of cultural, economic, and political exploitation must be taken seriously in human rights discussions, but the experience of colonialism should never become an excuse to curtail basic human rights on religious grounds.

A dialogical approach to comparative religious ethics provides a foundation for discussing the difficult but important subject of Islam and human rights. The presence of the language of human rights, which is alien to traditional Islamic sources such as the Qur'an, *sunna,* and *hadith,* and consensus on the importance of human rights among such otherwise diverse thinkers as Maududi, Qutb, and Soroush suggest that a degree of universalism concerning human rights is achievable. With the understanding that religion contributes in important and complementary ways to human rights debates, religious thought should enter into existing legal, political, and economic discourses on human rights.

The broader project of human rights and religion touches all citizens who live in diverse societies where people claim religious reasons for decisions that affect others. Although I began my study of Islam years prior to the attacks of September 11, 2001, that day and the events that continue to follow have lent an unanticipated urgency to the study of this religious tradition. In learning about Islam, as well as about any other religion that affects politics on a global level, we open up the possibility for respectful and informed dialogues. In demonstrating how Islamic scholars think about human rights, I hope to spark mutual understanding across religious, political, and cultural lines.

# —1—

# Conversations about Human Rights and Islam

The form of dialogue about human rights reflects the content of human rights. The way in which we converse about a topic affects the way in which we understand it. With regard to Islam and human rights, an approach to dialogue that is committed to understanding, openness, and fairness establishes necessary conditions for articulating universal norms of human rights. Unfortunately, such conversations about Islam and human rights have often been compromised by misperceptions of Islam, historical circumstance, and political considerations. Awareness of the way in which we come to such conversations, however, is an important first step toward establishing ideal conditions for dialogue.

## GADAMER AND CROSS-CULTURAL DIALOGUE

The approach to dialogue articulated by Gadamer adapts well to conversations among Islamic thinkers because they already share a familiarity with sacred scripture, religious jurisprudence, and other resources. The conversations among Maududi, Qutb, and Soroush, as well as other scholars of Islam, are facilitated by a shared familiarity with the larger history of Islam. Though they stand at different vantage points within a much greater tradition, the three identify themselves as Muslims living roughly within the same historical epoch. The conversations they have with each other through their scholarship are made within the context of a particular religious tradition, which encourages the discussion of certain subject matters.

Maududi, Qutb, and Soroush do not agree so much on particular judgments as they do on the issues within human rights that they deem important. Reading them collectively makes clear that some topics weigh far more heavily on their minds than others. Broad questions concerning the role of religion in political life, for example, and the relationship between the spiritual and the material, have occupied Islamic thinkers for centuries. More specific, but no less significant, questions about the requirements of democracy, the expression of divinely given conscience, and the place of tolerance in Islam have also inspired generations of religious scholars. They share religious resources that lead them to raise these issues and engage in dialogue about such matters as Muslims.

The hermeneutical theories of Gadamer appeal to a certain extent to thinkers such as Maududi, Qutb, and Soroush because they find that dialogue and progress require interactions with tradition. They each aim to acquire "the right horizon of inquiry for the questions evoked by the encounter with tradition." Gadamer explains that a horizon is a "range of vision that includes everything that can be seen from a particular vantage point."[1] Each vantage point leads to a particular view, a horizon. The familiarity among the three scholars with traditional Islamic resources such as the Qur'an, *sunna,* and *hadith* enables them to obtain similar, though not identical, horizons of inquiry regarding Islam and human rights.

Because each scholar stands at a different vantage point that changes with time, location, and numerous other factors, each holds a different perspective on the subject matter of Islam and its relationship to human rights. The Gadamerian idea of horizons suggests that distance and difference exist between one's vision and the visions of others. Maududi, Qutb, and Soroush face the difficulty, common to all, of writing out of several traditions or, in Gadamerian terms, with distinct prejudgments, because Muslims do not experience Islam as a singular, monolithic tradition and because they are not defined wholly by their religion.[2] Maududi, for example, speaks with an audience of subcontinental, formerly colonized Muslims in mind. Qutb writes out of a tradition specific to Sunni Islam, as well as one closely tied to the history of Egypt. Soroush draws not only on traditions found in Shi'ite Islam but also on Western philosophy, Persian history, and Muslim mystical poetry. The three thinkers articulate in their writings on Islam and human rights the differences between their visions and the visions of others, both Muslim and non-Muslim.

Conversation, although in many ways facilitated by a shared tradition, is nonetheless possible among persons with different points of view. Maududi, Qutb, and Soroush, because they share a religious tradition, are in several ways more capable of entering into a sustained dialogue about Islam and human rights. In spite of their shared identity as Muslims, however, the three hold substantive disagreements with each other. Their conversations reveal both the promises and difficulties of conversations with Muslims and non-Muslims about Islam and human rights.

Cross-cultural and interreligious dialogue, as well as comparative religious ethics, would benefit from Gadamer's approach to understanding. The application of Gadamer's ideas concerning hermeneutics to conversations about universal human rights clarifies both the process of dialogue and the subject matter of human rights. Because conversations about human rights and Islam face challenges associated with failures of understanding traditions in historical contexts, Gadamer's insights serve as an especially appropriate guide.

Gadamer attempts to revolutionize the field of hermeneutics by claiming that truths, which have traditionally been sought through scientific methods, can only be understood through a dialogical process that assumes the subjectivity of both the inquirer and the object of inquiry. He observes that the scientific methods of the past ask questions unidirectionally, that is, from the inquirer to the object of inquiry, and therefore are capable only of yielding information made possible by the creators of the methods themselves. An attitude of being open to unanticipated experiences is missing from this way of seeking knowledge.

Gadamer asserts that true understanding arises not from the imposition of a method onto an object, but rather from a dialectical process in which the "object" of inquiry also asks questions of the inquirer. Moreover, this dialogical process should not be viewed simply as a tool for humanistic understanding, but rather as the way in which humans actually exist in the world. The dialogical process, in other words, defines the being, the ontology, of humans.[3]

Primarily concerned with how we can understand history, Gadamer in *Truth and Method* describes how we in the present day might approach the past. He accepts that we are historically situated and laden with traditions that impose prejudgments on our views of any given situation.[4] Given this inescapable state of being, the only way in which we can understand the past is to broaden through dialogue what we know and then to distinguish between those presuppositions that help us to think and see more clearly and those that obscure our vision. Thus, although we necessarily exist in the world with prejudgments, those prejudgments can change over time through conversation.

Gadamer claims that we enter into human activity, into conversations, with an understanding of ourselves as historical beings with distinct vantage points. Although humans, each of whom is unique with an individual history, often fail to understand the views of other persons, conversations enable us to view the horizons of others who stand at different vantage points. Horizons fuse. Through conversations we may come to agreement on a subject matter.

Unavoidable differences among horizons, however, are not wholly incommensurable. Gadamer explains the importance of conversations for viewing and understanding the horizon of another, who stands at a different vantage point than one's own. He defines conversation as "a process of coming to an understanding. Thus it belongs to every true conversation that each person opens himself to the other, truly accepts his point of view as valid and transposes himself into the other to such an extent that he understands not the particular individual, but what he says. What is to be grasped is the substantive rightness of his opinion, so that we can be at one with each other on the subject. Thus we do not relate the other's opinion to him but to our own opinions and views."[5]

Conversation is a human, cognitive event that on occasion creates genuine understanding through the fusion of horizons on a particular subject matter.[6] When we converse with others, we are not attempting to understand our interlocutors as objects of inquiry, but we talk about subject matters of shared interest. Gadamer thus distinguishes between the understanding of a subject matter and the understanding of the individual. He is clear that, in a conversation, we are not primarily seeking to understand the person with whom we speak, but a third object, the subject matter.

The total independence of the subject matter from the individual, however, may be difficult to achieve. Indeed, because Gadamer claims that our knowledge of particular subject matters necessarily comes through the filter of our personal experiences, the idea of a subject matter wholly free of human imprint is inconceivable. Gadamer demands a kind of detachment from the subject matter, but in conversations about religious belief and ethical principles, such detachment may be nearly impossible. Nonetheless, such conversations about religion and ethics must occur out of necessity. Humans may never attain complete detachment from a subject matter, but they may proximate it. In the case of human rights, reminders of universal standards, not those standards that are applicable only to one's community, help to steer dialogue participants toward the kind of detachment that Gadamer's model demands. In conversations about human rights and religion, the primary subject matter for conversation concerns norms that are, or should be, shared universally.

Gadamer's dialogical approach to understanding further requires that persons enter into conversations freely. True understanding does not take place under conditions of coercion. He explains that where "a person is concerned with the other as individuality—e.g., in a therapeutic conversation or the interrogation of a man accused of a crime—this is not really a situation in which two people are trying to come to an understanding."[7] Implied in this distinction and in the examples that Gadamer provides is the notion of equality between participants. In a therapy session or criminal interrogation, there often exists a power imbalance between the person who wants to obtain information and the person who may hold it. The patient and the accused are not equally participating in the understanding of the subject matter. Indeed, the subject matter and the participant, that is, the interrogated, are inseparable. Persons being interrogated may likely be engaged in the "conversation" against their will.

The distinction between a true conversation and one that is forced requires that distinctions be made between conversations about human rights violations and those about determining human rights standards. A "conversation" about human rights violations in which one participant stands accused of humanitarian crimes would probably not meet the criterion of free and willing participation. A conversation concerning the content of human rights in which participants exchange ideas and are valued for their opinions, however, would far more likely be characterized by the attitude of openness so important to Gadamer's dialogical model of understanding.

Admittedly, conversation and understanding have proved difficult when Muslim thinkers and non-Muslim thinkers enter into conversations about the role of religion in human rights. Although such conversations are not coercive in the same way that a "conversation" between a police officer and an accused criminal might be, a definite power imbalance marks conversations between representatives of the United States and Western Europe on the one hand and Muslim-majority nations on the other. Because of this reality, the critiques of Habermas are indispensable for reframing Gadamer's otherwise appropriate approach to dialogue.

## CORRECTING DISTORTED DIALOGUE: HABERMAS

The famous debates between Gadamer and Habermas revolve primarily around the question of whether truth can emerge through the dialogical process itself or whether the uncovering of truth requires a critical perspective external to the dialogue. Considering Gadamer's insistence on the inescapability of tradition, Habermas challenges the optimistic belief that dialogue can escape traditions' ideological constraints. These ideological constraints are both profound and systematic; they affect the very nature of interpretation and dialogue. The objects of our interpretation possess histories of interpretations, and those histories, in turn, produce effects on future interpretations. Histories create ideologies through which we view the world. Some historical effects and ideologies that affect our interpretative acts are relatively innocuous. For example, we perceive a flat rectangular object with a textured image on a wall as a painting and analyze it as such because we come to the object from within a tradition that tells us that this is a piece of art to be viewed. We have, even before we analyze the painting, already committed an act of interpretation. We have interpreted the object on the wall as a painting, and we approach the painting as tradition has deemed appropriate (i.e., we look at the painting but do not touch, smell, or taste it). This object on the wall possesses a history of interpretation, which affects future interpretations. Generations past have interpreted, and future generations will interpret, the object in question as a painting.

As demonstrated in the example above, not all historical effects of tradition are necessarily negative, but some historical effects can be. Ideologies that objectify people, whether of a different ethnicity, sex, or age, have, for example, led to countless examples of oppressive and inhumane treatment. Under such circumstances, "normal communication," wherein people can clarify misunderstandings, faces tremendous obstacles.[8] Situations of extreme power imbalances, such as those found under conditions of slavery, genocide, and colonialism, indicate that the oppressor does not even recognize the object of oppression as possessing a legitimate voice for correcting injustices. The oppressed may not perceive themselves as capable of engaging as equals in dialogue with their oppressors. No genuine conversation can begin; indeed, interlocutors may not even notice the abnormality of communication. These communication disturbances, Habermas argues, are especially insidious due to their systematic nature. As noted by Susan Shapiro, they are "built into the very activity of interpretation . . . for certain ends or because of certain motives." Moreover, these negative effects "are not the result of misinterpretation or a misunderstanding. Rather these negative effects are carried, as it were, by the tradition, by the conversation itself."[9] Dialogue alone cannot correct these deeply entrenched negative effects found within the hermeneutical act.

Habermas labels the incorporation of negative effects into the very act of interpretation as "systematically distorted communication."[10] Systematically distorted communication results from the confusion between "actions oriented to reaching understanding" and "actions oriented to success."[11] This abnormal form of communication arises specifically when strategic actions taken to ensure "success," in contrast to ensuring understanding, are both concealed and unconscious. This analysis, when applied to a context of oppression, suggests that both the oppressor and the oppressed are unaware of the distortions in communication.[12] Because all participants do not perceive these distortions, dialogue, which takes place on the level of consciousness, is of no help in correcting misunderstandings.

In order to escape systematically distorted communication, one needs to move beyond conscious dialogue into an analysis of the unconscious. Habermas specifically advocates the use of Freudian psychoanalysis to undo the ideological repression that distorts communication.[13] The therapist acts as a neutral third-party observer, who stands outside of the dialogue and is able to view the dialogue from a nonbiased, rational perspective. Because ideologies are so deeply entrenched in our communicative acts, only the intervention of a neutral observer can correct the systematic distortions found in dialogue.

When systematic distortions have been corrected, conditions are set for the creation of an "ideal speech situation." In an ideal speech situation, systematic distortions do not hinder dialogue. Both internal constraints, in the form of ideologically based repression, and external constraints, in the form of power imbalances, are absent. Dialogue would take place in the absence of "open domination, conscious strategic behavior, or the more subtle barriers to communication deriving from self-deception."[14] Participants in dialogue share equal opportunities to speak, and their roles in dialogue are balanced. This "general symmetry requirement" outlines the rules of dialogue that would characterize the ideal speech situation. Participants would possess the same ability to initiate and continue dialogue, to assert ideas, and to challenge others' assertions. All ideas, regardless of their origins, would be open to critique and scrutiny.

The significance of the ideal speech situation to Habermas's ethics lies in the belief that only under conditions of equality and freedom can true consensus occur. For Habermas, genuine consensus does not lie in the mere overlapping of similar perceptions but in a rational consensus free of illusions. This is a consensus with which any "rational, competent judge" would concur.[15] Under the conditions of the ideal speech situation, only the better argument, not the stronger debater, prevails. The cooperation of the participants works solely to render the best ideas, not to reinforce existing power imbalances. In the case of human rights, the ideal speech situation would enable participants to come to a consensus about human rights norms without psychologically repressed ideologies or the presuppositions of existing political relations. The force of the idea of human rights, not extraneous concerns, would dominate the conversation.

Habermas recognizes that the ideal speech situation is not realistic.[16] Given the fact of historically entrenched differences in power and the probable existence of systematically distorted communication, ideal speech situations would be rare, if not nonexistent. One might also note that the introduction of the liberating psychotherapist who is both human and yet somehow free of ideology stretches the imagination. Indeed, Freudian psychotherapy itself might be considered an ideological shackle tainted by cultural, historical, and sexist bias. Habermas maintains, however, that the recognition of the ideal speech situation serves as a valuable supposition to discourse. The ideal speech situation functions as a guide against which conversations can be measured. As a guide, it could help to improve discourse or to illuminate underlying conditions of discourse that compromise the ideal speech situation. In human rights discourse, the ideal speech situation performs the critical task of illuminating power imbalances among participants. It places into question the conditions under which existing human rights norms were created and demands sensitivity to differences in the perception of human rights on the basis of cultural and historical backgrounds.

Critics of Habermas, including Karl-Otto Apel and Dietrich Böhler, argue that he too easily conflates theoretical reflection with practical engagement. Emancipation in the realm of reflection and theory should not be confused with political and economic emancipation. Although our unconscious may be liberated, this does not necessarily translate into the liberation of people in the material world. Habermas's identification of self-reflection and psychotherapy with practical ethics has been criticized as "a simple identification" and "an idealist illusion."[17]

For Böhler, Habermas's freedom from the suppressed unconscious does not necessitate practical engagement. He sees Habermas's uniting of formal theory with practical engagement as "an undigested Fichtean moment" characterized by self-interest that serves as the ground for all other interests.[18] In particular, Habermas's equating of freedom with the disillusion of dogmatism dismisses other views of emancipation and self-reflection. This critique is especially applicable to religious believers who understand God, not self-reflection through psychotherapy, as the source of emancipation and who may not view freedom from the "ideology" of religion as desirable. Practical engagement for religious believers may not be motivated by emancipation from ideology but rather the very result of religious ideology.

In spite of these criticisms, Habermas's ideas concerning discourse, particularly the identification of systematically distorted communication and the ideal speech situation, provide valuable tools for human rights theory. Because universal human rights norms develop out of dialogue with persons representing groups from relative situations of power, Habermas's views bring into focus those power differentials.

Viewed through this lens, a document such as the UDHR appears in a new light. The UN General Assembly debates that took place in the months leading up to the December 1948 passage of the UDHR involved not only the world's colonizers but also newly independent nations, including many Muslim-majority ones.[19] Although clear and noncontroversial consensus did emerge on a number of human rights norms, one can see, on closer examination of those debates, that many articles presented genuine conflicts to marginalized groups. These fledgling nations, unsurprisingly, lost the debates to more powerful nations and their allies. The UDHR as ratified contains neither references to the power struggles evident during those debates nor any indication of those nations that won those debates. Power imbalances, as found between colonizing nations and their former colonies, affect the conditions of discourse as well as any resulting consensus concerning human rights norms. The norms that receive the label "universal" may, in fact, not be universal at all. The consensus on human rights norms may have been forced as a result of systematically distorted communication. Agreement over universal human rights norms would not have been achieved under an ideal speech situation, and perhaps not even with an awareness of a comparative ideal.

Habermas's insights supplement Gadamer's theories of dialogue by drawing attention to the conditions under which horizons seemingly fuse. Although Gadamer's approach to dialogue applies more readily to human rights discourse in that it assumes, unlike Habermas, the persistence of traditions and prejudgments among interlocutors, it does not offer an explicit awareness of these traditions and prejudgments as enabling the perpetuation of unequal power relations. Habermas's suspicions play against Gadamer's optimism in dialogue. In the case of Islamic thinkers as participants in conversations about human rights, Gadamer would welcome the insights of religious tradition and prejudgments, whereas Habermas would bring out the distortions in communication arising from both religious ideology and political repression. If Islamic thinkers moreover represent postcolonial peoples, Habermas would be especially wary of a fusion of horizons concerning human rights, particularly in the presence of continued political, economic, and social inequality. In bringing together the thoughts of Gadamer and Habermas on dialogue and understanding, one can increase sensitivity to both religious views and political contexts.

The ideas of Gadamer and Habermas provide necessary correctives for the other. Whereas Gadamer makes possible—and hopeful—understanding across divides of tradition and history, Habermas helps to ensure that understanding occurs under just circumstances. The balance of the two is especially important when one discusses the pressing but contentious issue of Islamic views on human rights. Conversations about human rights must take place if we are at all concerned about the well-being of others, but such conversations are fraught with political, historical, and cultural tensions. Particularly when representatives of Western nations characterize Islam as inimical to human rights, members of Muslim-majority nations who suffered under Western colonialism are bound to see such accusations as hypocritical, at the very least. Whether assessments of Islam as hostile to human rights are accurate would be difficult to determine under such circumstances. Especially because Islam in recent years has become the focus of attention with regard to major human rights violations, the need for open, fair, and critical discussion is clear.

Given the diversity of religious traditions, and the diversity within each tradition, a number of different vantage points and horizons exist with which to consider human rights. Although non-Muslim thinkers may not grasp Muslim religious sources as readily as Muslims, certain subject matters, in addition to the broader topic of human rights, emerge across traditions. Conversations such as those that took place during the creation of the UDHR were the first steps toward understanding and agreement on the substantive rightness of important subject matters. In drafting the UDHR, not only a diversity of Muslims but also a range of religious and philosophical thinkers representing a number of different traditions were able to agree on the need to uphold human rights universally. More specifically, they agreed on the importance—even if they were not able to agree on the details—of issues such as democracy, toleration, and freedom of conscience as human rights. These subjects functioned, and continue to function, as mediating topics of conversation and, possibly, understanding. Moreover, these subjects still serve as the basis from which to interrogate the universality of human rights claims from multiple perspectives. Among Islamic thinkers and with thinkers from outside Islam, the discourse of human rights provides significant opportunities for cross-cultural conversations about the possibility of a universal ethic.

## DENYING OPEN DISCOURSE: THE PROBLEM OF FOUNDATIONLESS HUMAN RIGHTS

Although the international scale of the human rights project demonstrates that the instigators of the UDHR earnestly attempted to include non-Western voices, they were nonetheless products of their time. The majority of the leaders of the human rights effort in the late 1940s were Western-educated white men of privilege from Europe and the United States. They guided an effort that remained in its overall structure a product of their beliefs and imagination, even if along the way they sought input from delegates of non-Western nations. To be sure, the gist of the declaration was heralded by virtually all participating nations, but the details of the declaration, spelled out in thirty articles, have remained controversial.

Since the creation of the UDHR, various human rights theorists have tried to clarify human rights because they found the original document unwieldy, inadequate, or otherwise incapable of motivating progress globally. They all agree that current articulations of human rights could be improved, but disagree as to how. One area of debate among these thinkers concerns the role of religion in human rights. Not surprisingly, several theorists find that religion frustrates human rights efforts and recommend that human rights projects not involve religion at all. Ignatieff, for example, states unequivocally that religion must be left out of human rights discussions because it serves only as an obstacle to human rights. Other human rights thinkers offer frameworks that enable the blending of religious belief with human rights efforts.[20]

Theorists such as Ignatieff argue that persons of differing faith traditions can best achieve human rights by focusing on the practical and political aspects of human rights. He argues for a foundationless or nonfoundational conception of human rights, specifically, one that does not rely on religious or philosophical grounds for the existence of those rights.[21] Compared to foundational models of human rights, which he believes seem divisive at best and offensive at worst, a foundationless theory based on human experiences, rather than religious belief, appears more likely to garner unilateral support. For pragmatic reasons, Ignatieff and other secular thinkers assert that human rights should not focus on philosophical or religious issues. According to Ignatieff, empathy based on the common human experience of fear and the belief that persons should not have to live in fear serves as compelling enough reasons for human rights.[22]

Nonetheless, if one major goal of theorists such as Ignatieff consists of garnering the support, generation, and enforcement of human rights by religious populations, then they should consider the possibility of constructing a model of human rights that accommodates a variety of foundations rather than none at all. Enforcement of human rights will likely fail unless people find compelling reasons for the practice of human rights. As K. Anthony Appiah contends, "Without some grounding—metaphysical or not—it is hard to see why [human rights instruments] should have any power or effect."[23] For many people around the world, particular religious beliefs provide the primary and sustained motivating basis for human rights. A foundationless model of human rights or, rather, a model based solely on faith in human agency, has failed and will continue to fail in persuading religious believers—particularly those who have experienced the direct harms of unmitigated human agency.

Theorists who advocate a nonreligious approach to human rights find foundationless models more attractive than religious ones in part due to an incomplete understanding of religious beliefs and traditions. Although they realize that Muslims, like Christians, express their belief in God through a variety of ways and that internal disagreement exists within larger traditions, they nonetheless describe religious conviction as limiting human dignity rather than inspiring activism. Ignatieff, for example, acknowledges that religion has at times improved the human condition, such as in the case of the civil rights movement, but finds such examples insufficient to counter the advantages of a foundationless framework for human rights. He writes that "the religious side believes that only if humans get down on their knees can they save themselves from their own destructiveness; a humanist believes that they will do so only if they stand up on their own two feet." Nonreligious theorists may perceive that religion imposes "a limit on the human will to power."[24] This claim, although perhaps convincing to other nonreligious theorists, would be quickly qualified by scholars, theologians, and religious believers as but one of many views of religion.[25]

Maududi, Qutb, and Soroush would certainly disagree with Ignatieff that religion is impractical for achieving human rights. Ignatieff's comments on religion grossly oversimplify the complex relationship among Islam, human rights, and just action. If anything, Maududi, Qutb, and Soroush argue that Islam provides an awareness of the issues of material and social equality that other belief systems do not provide. Although Maududi explicitly states that material and social equity between the West and Muslims will be achieved if Muslims become better believers, he does not think that people become better believers by, as Ignatieff suggests, simply getting "down on their knees."[26] Indeed, the strategies for promoting human rights offered by the range of Islamic thinkers require vigorous collective efforts to organize effective governments, create supporting institutions, and advance technologically. None of these religiously inspired projects displays the quietism that Ignatieff finds in religious belief.

The gap between nonfoundationalists, such as Ignatieff, and religious thinkers can be bridged with a greater consideration of the assumptions of religion and human nature that form the basis of their theories.[27] The fear that religion aids in oppressing the weak assumes that religion functions in all cases to quell the ego, greed, and quests for power. Lessons such as "the meek shall inherit the earth" teach the oppressed that they should not demand justice and that if they continue in their quiet suffering, they shall be rewarded in the afterlife. This is exactly the message that poor and underprivileged religious people do not need. If anything, the critics of religion argue, the powerless need to assert themselves and demand material justice and greater power. Human rights activists and thinkers with this view of religion are sure to denounce religious belief. Given such perceptions of religion, they would understandably argue for a nonfoundational, nonreligious framework for human rights.

Fortunately, many religious thinkers, particularly those writing after colonialism and after World War II, recognize the importance of addressing the concerns of the weaker members of society from the perspective of the marginalized. The Holocaust and the aftermath of colonization have demanded reformulations of religious belief in order to attend better to the needs of the oppressed and powerless. Indebted partially to liberation theologies and feminist scholarship, religious thinkers of various traditions who emerge after this time critique and expand traditional views of religion and human nature.[28] Activists ranging from Gandhi to Martin Luther King Jr., as well as such thinkers as Maududi and Qutb, view religion as a source of strength for the downtrodden. They speak not only to the powerful, for whom religious teachings serve as a reminder to be more humble, but also to the powerless, for whom religious teachings serve as an inspiration to seek justice.

Foundationless human rights thinkers overlook the inherently interpretive and responsive nature of religions. The support of human rights found in major world religions today, notably through the inclusion of human rights into the thinking of even traditionalist conservative Islamic scholars, indicates the responsiveness of religious thought to larger human developments. The creation of the UIDHR in 1981 attests to the ability and desire among Islamic political leaders to adopt human rights, even if the UIDHR contains elements that are clearly problematic for other human rights theorists and activists.[29] Moreover, the plethora of liberal thinkers within Islam, such as Soroush, as well as within other world religions, should reassure nonfoundational thinkers of the compatibility between human rights and religious belief. Champions of foundationless human rights models, in considering religion as interpretive and responsive, should accommodate foundational beliefs for human rights.

To assume that religious thinkers support human rights causes is both warranted and practical. Because people will likely continue to perceive, deliberate, and act as religious citizens, human rights thinkers will find more success in accommodating religious beliefs to further their goals rather than in pushing these beliefs aside. By asking religious believers to suppress religious identities when discussing fundamental human needs and freedoms, secular human rights thinkers, in their failure to accept religious believers on their own terms, risk alienating the populations they hope to help. The most pragmatic way to ensure universal human rights lies in the acceptance of foundational beliefs in human rights thought.

## CONTINUING THE CONVERSATION: DISCUSSING RELIGIOUS DUTY

One possible way to begin discussions on the role of religion in human rights efforts is to reconsider the universal language of duty. Duties, as Jack Donnelly reminds us, are not and should not be confused with rights. Rights are tools given to the oppressed; duties are the obligations of the privileged. With this distinction in mind, rights nonetheless lack significance if no one accepts the duty to aid those whose rights have been violated. The rights of the oppressed, although they can always be claimed, cannot be realized or restored unless those who are in a position to help believe that they have a duty to do so.[30]

Human rights, as Henry Shue points out, always require correlative duties.[31] Regardless of whether a community grounds human rights in secular liberalism or in traditionalist Islam, a community must address the subject of duty if it commits to upholding human rights. Because religious traditions, including Islam, often emphasize duty as part of religious practice, exploring the topic of duty potentially offers areas of overlapping concern on the topic of human rights between communities that otherwise seem to support divergent values.

Political theorists, including human rights thinkers, often accommodate religious reasoning in the public sphere by separating it from political reasoning and focusing on areas of overlapping political consensus. Theorists' attempts to separate the political from the religious, however, reject the worldview of Muslim thinkers who maintain that political commitments exist inseparably from religious belief. Rather than assume a distinction between the religious and the political, especially one that privileges the political over the religious in pluralistic communities, participants in dialogue should focus on finding common subject matters. Although the discourse that then takes place may include religious explication, it should still remain focused on the common subject. Religious reasoning may enter into the conversation. The participants in the discussion have the agency to determine the necessity of using religious language when discussing the common subject; if necessary, they may also have to explain the necessity of using religious language. Although this process may prove less expedient than the Rawlsian model of overlapping political consensus, it avoids discriminating against religious thinkers whose comprehensive views disallow the separation of the political from the sacred.

In contrast to Shue, thinkers such as Donnelly and Ignatieff do not see religious traditions as contributing significantly to human rights.[32] They dangerously ignore the persistence and importance of religion in crafting values necessary for the propagation and enforcement of human rights. Required of these thinkers is a reimagining of religious traditionalism rather than its dismissal. Although Donnelly argues that traditional cultures lack the foundations for the exercise of correlative duties, much less human rights, he concedes that correlative duties can play a significant role in the establishment of rights. Donnelly believes that if persons are to attain full human dignity, all human rights should be considered basic. Shue, by contrast, argues that few "basic" rights, namely, the rights to security, subsistence, and liberty, are required if persons are to enjoy other rights. Moreover, these rights necessarily bear correlative duties.

Shue argues in favor of correlative duties basic to human rights by demonstrating first that the traditional distinction between negative and positive rights describes situations inaccurately. The right to security, for instance, although traditionally viewed as a negative right, realistically requires a number of positive duties. In order to enable persons to exercise the right to security, people need to create police forces, criminal judicial systems, jails and prisons, and so forth. The right to subsistence, although traditionally viewed as a positive right, may, on the other hand, require very few positive duties. The distinction between "negative" and "positive," as Shue suggests, may be more usefully applied to duties rather than to rights.

For every basic "right" there exist three correlative duties. The right to security, for example, requires that the state or ruling body accept the duties to (a) not eliminate a person's security, (b) protect people from the deprivation of security by other people, and (c) provide for the security of those unable to provide for their own.[33] Similarly, the right to subsistence requires that one accept the duties to (a) avoid eliminating a person's only available means of subsistence, (b) protect people against deprivation by other people of the only available means of subsistence, and (c) provide for the subsistence of those unable to provide for their own. The three correlative duties to any basic right can be summarized as (a) the duty to avoid depriving, (b) the duty to protect from deprivation, and (c) the duty to aid the deprived.

A governing body cannot guarantee rights unless it also upholds the three correlative duties. The usual excuses for not supporting human rights, particularly those excuses that depend on the distinction between negative and positive rights, no longer seem valid. This line of reasoning resonates with religious thinkers who emphasize the moral obligations of a ruler toward the people.

The duties that religious thinkers claim to be rights, however, Donnelly finds "neither derivative from nor correlative to human rights."[34] Nonetheless, the examples of traditional duties Donnelly provides appear broad enough in scope that one can translate them into rights and correlative duties. Religions are, after all, inherently interpretive, so although Donnelly would be right to point out that traditional religious texts often fail to include the specific term "rights," the significance of those distinctions is not as detrimental as he portends. Both the religious motivation and the extrapolation of the human rights concept remain despite the lack of the literal evidence in texts such as the Bible and Qur'an. Equally important, the acknowledged interpreters of divine scripture, including the Qur'an, themselves use the language of human rights when discussing the application of Qur'anic principles to the contemporary age.

In the case of Islam, Donnelly worries that "scriptural passages cited as establishing a right to protection of life are in fact divine injunctions not to kill and to consider life as inviolable."[35] Traditions of scriptural interpretation found in text-based religions, however, allow, if not encourage, the translation of divine injunctions such as the one cited above into practical rules of living, including the ability to appeal to rights and the demand for correlative duties. Divine injunctions not to kill and to consider life as inviolable can be understood as (a) the duty to avoid depriving, (b) the duty to protect from deprivation, and (c) the duty to aid the deprived.

Donnelly underutilizes the power of scriptural interpretation and the theological tools that make coherent a statement such as "human rights in Islam are the privilege of God, because authority ultimately belongs to him." He finds the previous statement "quite literally incoherent: 'human rights' . . . are not rights of human beings but privileges of God."[36] He does not acknowledge that in Islam (or, for that matter, in Christianity and Judaism), there exists the idea of *imago dei*, the imprint of God found in each human being. Humans must express their reverence for God "horizontally," that is, through their correct relationships with other humans in society if they are to express their reverence for God "vertically." The "privilege" of God could thus be interpreted as that aspect of divinity to be found and respected in each human being, including oneself. Donnelly characterizes religious statements as incoherent only because he does not interpret them through the lens of theological, cultural, or religious tradition. Interpreted in the appropriate context, such statements provide grounds for human rights and correlative duties.[37] The notions of *taqwa* and *hidaya*, which are akin to the notion of *imago dei* and function as conscience in Islamic thought, are the religious bases for respecting freedom of conscience and tolerating religious difference.[38] *Taqwa* and *hidaya* represent the divine spark, found in every human, that provides moral guidance. Precisely because this inner spark is considered divine, and not wholly human, are the conscience and freedom of belief protected in Islam.[39] This oversight on the part of Donnelly can probably be attributed to other human rights thinkers who too quickly dismiss the complexity of theological ideas.

Maududi and Qutb find no difficulty applying the religious notion of duty to human rights. Although their restrictions on toleration and freedom of conscience pose difficulties, they nonetheless assert that governments have a religious duty to ensure some level of freedom, security, and subsistence. The frequently quoted Qur'anic command to enjoin good and forbid evil forms the foundation of many of their ideas on governance, toleration, and freedom of conscience. Qutb, in particular, makes clear that the needy have a right to *zakat,* or alms given by the better-off members of society, and that both governments and the wealthy possess the correlative duty to provide subsistence to their people. If anything, Qutb overemphasizes the right of the poor to take *zakat* and proclaims that the poor have the duty themselves to lay claims to charitable funds. Maududi, Qutb, and Soroush extend the idea of subsistence to the infrastructure necessary to establish and maintain a democratic government. Governments must establish schools, hospitals, and other institutions that they believe make democracy possible; the people have an uncontestable right to demand this of their leaders.

With regard to security, Maududi and Qutb believe that a government's duty lies beyond freedom from bodily harm. A government that claims to abide by Islamic law should provide moral security for the people. They believe that Western governments do not pay enough attention to protecting the spiritual and emotional health of its citizens. Muslims, and people generally, are entitled to live in an emotionally and spiritually healthy environment. The controversy that arises, especially with regard to the ideas of Maududi and Qutb, concerns not whether the duty to ensure security exists, but the limits of that duty. Although their advocacy of toleration and religious freedom helps to balance their restrictively protectionist stances, their ideas nonetheless suffer from an uneasy tension between freedom and security. In the eyes of many Western human rights theorists, an Islạmic government's duty to provide security and liberty infringes unacceptably on the freedoms that human rights should protect.

These concerns are valid, but the larger point that Shue makes about the place of duty in ensuring human rights still holds. Employing the framework and language of duty plausibly extends the legitimacy of human rights into cultures where people invoke the language of duty more frequently than rights. Maududi and Qutb move comfortably between the terms of duty and rights within the realm of religious tradition and make clear that the language of duty in scripture manifests itself as rights.

Donnelly's argument denies the possibility of developing human rights in non-Western, non-Christian cultures in an attempt to prove the validity of a universalist history, which reaches its apex in the paradigm of Western civilization. He not only restricts the potential of the idea of correlative duties and rights but also suggests that the only culture capable of properly developing human rights is the Western, liberal one.[40] Granted that the philosophical and political idea of rights did originate in Western European culture, this does not preclude the ability of non-Westerners to adopt the idea and language of rights. Living cultures and societies are dynamic; over time, they adopt and incorporate ideas that originated elsewhere.[41] Soroush points out that the leaders of the Iranian Revolution were themselves inspired by political ideals that originated in Western Europe. Likewise, powerful ideas such as feminism and Marxism, in addition to major world religions, have been adopted globally. The argument does not hold that only the originators of an idea are best capable of bringing that idea to fruition—that, for example, only Christians living in biblical lands are most capable of living as Christians. Ideas, including the idea of human rights, will certainly change, though not necessarily for the worst, depending on the context in which people receive them.

The concept of correlative duties provides a means for cultures to adapt human rights into preexisting ethical and political structures. This concept presents a potentially effective strategy for encouraging the development of human rights in other cultures, particularly those that appear to emphasize duties and obligations over what we might consider to be rights. The emphasis on taking responsibility for others can function as a powerful motivational tool for human rights activity. Furthermore, in some situations, human rights movements must begin with a duty or obligation to others. The process of educating the victimized so that they are able to claim rights from governments begins with an obligation on behalf of the educated to the victims.[42] A necessary first step in securing human rights may entail appeals to those who have the obligation—and the power—to make changes. If the source of those obligations, and the power to fulfill them, originates in religious belief, then human rights thinkers and activists need to ally themselves with religious believers to promote shared visions of justice.

## A MINIMALIST APPROACH TO UNIVERSAL HUMAN RIGHTS

The inclusion of religious reasoning in human rights dialogue raises the concern that universal human rights will skew toward unacceptably oppressive conservatism and traditionalism, especially with the inclusion of Islamic thought. This would be the case under two conditions: first, if Islam were oppressively conservative and traditionalist, and second, if universal human rights were the result of an average or median of existing ethics. The first condition can be dismissed with the recognition of tremendous diversity and complexity within Islam. Radically liberal and strictly conservative Muslims sit as bookends to the wide variety of religious and political thought contained within Islam. Even those Islamic thinkers viewed as conservative and traditionalist are not predictably so with regard to their ideas concerning human rights. The characterization of material and institutional rights and obligations within the writings of Maududi and Qutb, for example, might be viewed as socialist or communist.

The second condition concerns the method of deriving human rights. The recognition of religious groups as legitimate partners in human rights triggers the fear that any declaration of universal human rights will be skewed as a result of their participation. The perception that Islam oppresses women, for instance, leads to the concern that if Islamic societies have an equal say in determining universal human rights, their participation will compromise a strong global statement on human rights for women. This is a legitimate concern, particularly for those human rights that are considered more negotiable and less important than others. Governments would not likely indulge a nation that approved of genocide by removing protection from genocide from a list of universal human rights, but they might reconsider a statement on women's rights if it offended too many participating governments.[43]

Although human rights should not fall prey to arguments for cultural deference, the pretense that human rights come out of nowhere is surely false. The concept of human rights traces its genealogy to Western liberalism and is endorsed today by many non-Western, nonliberal cultures. Moreover, as human rights have evolved over the last several decades, non-Western societies have contributed to the refinement of universal human rights. Some aspects of human rights remain in appearance more Western than others, but the general concept of human rights finds acceptance virtually everywhere. The difficulty lies in determining those aspects of human rights that contain universal value and transcend conventional moralities, despite the fact that our best guess of universal values comes out of our knowledge of existing ethical standards. To promote universalism in human rights means agreeing on those rights or entitlements that anyone, anywhere, anytime should be able to claim as a necessary condition for human dignity that others have a duty to protect. For Western societies in dialogue with Islamic ones, overcoming the difficulties of cross-cultural dialogue requires both commitment to universal human rights and a self-critique of the values that enabled imperialism and its deleterious effects on a global scale. With regard to Islamic societies, this entails separating universal values from dubious postcolonial political strategies and specious cultural practices cloaked in religious language. Both Western and Islamic societies must share the vision of articulating those conditions necessary for human dignity that the oppressed can claim and that others can and should provide.

The conditions necessary for human dignity are notoriously difficult to formulate as a statement of human rights. Long lists of rights, such as the UDHR, contain controversial social and economic rights that detract from ostensibly more fundamental rights. Shorter lists, such as Shue's list of three basic rights, fail to capture the comprehensive quality of human rights. Other formulations, such as Rawls's notion of "decency" as the normative standard for human rights, rely ultimately on an unenforceable intuitive grasp of justice and moral imperative.[44] The frailties of human understanding and the historicized lens through which we might comprehend human rights render any statement susceptible to flaws. The survival of human rights as a universal ethic beyond such inevitable obstacles depends on continuous and open global discussion.[45] The responsibilities of Western societies and Islamic ones therefore include attempts not only to distinguish their own unique particularities from universal values but also to contribute to human rights dialogue with a spirit of perpetuating discussion.

Minimalist approaches to human rights invite dialogue between Western and Islamic societies more effectively than more comprehensive approaches. A minimalist approach focuses on a few rights without the details found in fuller accounts of human rights. These rights, which must exemplify the quality of universalism, are in theory easier to agree on as universal values compared to peripheral or supporting ideas found in more comprehensive approaches, which are more likely to reflect particular cultural norms. The right to participate in one's government, for example, is far more likely to garner agreement as a universal human right than, for example, the right to marry without regard to race, religion, or sexual orientation. Declaring as a human right certain conditions of marriage—the issues of child marriage and domestic violence aside—imparts the flavor to human rights overall as a project of Western cultural imperialism. Equally important, a minimalist approach to human rights avoids asserting rights that provide formerly colonized societies an excuse for rejecting human rights altogether as the latest form of Western cultural imperialism.

A minimalist approach, however, should not provide justification to avoid interference by or in another state should some violation of human rights occur.[46] In other words, governments should not dismiss certain human rights because of the fear that such rights would invite scrutiny or because of the belief that interventions taken to protect that right would be interpreted as imperialistic. Given the situation where a Muslim nation denies, for example, interreligious marriage, this nation might argue that such unions do not constitute a universal human right but is simply a form of Western imperialism. Other nations may fear being labeled imperialist if they intervene to protect interreligious marriage as a human right.[47] If governments by and large agree, even with few detractors, that interreligious marriage is a genuinely universal human right, that is, a condition necessary for human dignity that others can and should protect, then intervention—though not necessarily a military one—would be justified and cannot rightly be labeled imperialist.[48] A minimalist approach would not prevent the declaration or protection of a universal human right simply because the right might be perceived as an excuse for imperialist activity.

For Islamic societies whose citizens' memories of Western imperialism make difficult the separation of universal human rights from protectionist arguments for "tradition," the value of continued dialogue cannot be overestimated. The broad acceptance of human rights within Islamic societies and the variety within Islamic thought bode well for the ultimate success of dialogue both across religious lines and within Islamic societies. Moreover, the principle within Islamic law that errs toward the granting of freedom, rather than its restriction, aligns with the importance of protecting freedoms within human rights.[49] For example, if we look at the issue of women's suffrage, which is currently denied in Saudi Arabia, we find that dialogue within and among Islamic governments has proved effective. The decision in May 2005 by Kuwaiti legislators to grant women the right to vote resulted in large part from the results of a three-decade-long intra-Muslim debate about the status of women's rights in Islam.

Human rights provide the motivation for governments to establish the legislative and institutional structures required for human dignity. Once governments provide those laws and institutions, people can choose whether to take advantage of those opportunities. Interference that denies the decisions of competent and consenting adults differs from interference in the affairs of another state to protect human rights. If a nation allows women to vote, but women choose not to exercise their vote, then intervention would not be justified. No universal human right has been violated. The capabilities approach applied to human rights, illustrated by Martha Nussbaum, helps to clarify this important distinction.[50] With a focus on a spectrum of human functions, the capabilities approach directs human rights thinkers and activists toward the opportunities that enable persons to make choices that allow for human flourishing, rather than the choices made with those opportunities. An ascetic chooses to limit food intake to achieve spiritual enlightenment; a starving person makes no such choice. To interfere with the decision of the ascetic by forcing him to eat would be strongly and unjustifiably paternalistic, but to place food in the hands of the starving person would not be unjustified, even though such action may be characterized as weakly paternalistic.

In comparison to Nussbaum's list of capabilities, minimalist human rights formulations limit the range of human rights to those that can be fulfilled as a duty or obligation. Hence, the right to subsistence can be protected by others, but what Nussbaum describes as the capability "to have attachments to things and people outside ourselves," although possibly important for human dignity, cannot be protected or granted fully by others.[51] The capability to have attachments might translate into the protection of freedom from excessive trauma, fear, and anxiety, which would likely interfere in the development of healthy relationships; however, such a capability generally would be difficult to render into a duty to be assumed by others should the need arise. Amartya Sen reasons that some plausible rights, such as the "right to tranquility," should be excluded as a human right despite its potential significance because of "the difficulty of guaranteeing it through social help."[52] Minimalist approaches to human rights limit rights to those that others can perceive as a duty that can be fulfilled. Some examples of human rights that would be included in a minimalist approach are as follows: (a) freedom from torture; (b) clean water and adequate food; (c) basic education; (d) participation in government; and (e) freedom of speech and assembly.

Minimizing human rights to those rights that others can secure or protect, incorporating the distinctions between capabilities and decisions, and distinguishing those rights that possess the quality of universalism advance the project of human rights. These standards for a minimalist approach to human rights aim to perpetuate conversation among and with people whose perspectives are too easily dismissed as incompatible. A cross-cultural, interreligious dialogue about human rights might begin with a right that is generally considered unassailable, such as the right to freedom from torture. Moving toward understanding, and eventually toward agreement, should begin with precedent conversations that set up the possibility for understanding and agreement. Although disagreements will inevitably arise, the moral exercise of accepting one's interlocutors as agents with reasons, traditions, and histories is valuable in and of itself.

Among the more difficult conversations may be those with Muslims who present views that initially seem incommensurable with one's own. Nonetheless, Islamic voices, particularly those that represent the frustrations echoed in reactionary statements, must be included in global dialogues with Western governments on human rights. To dismiss the participation of religious thinkers completely because of the distrust generated by religious extremists would in essence allow the extremists to define religion under their terms. Careful and broad-minded perspectives on Islam, rather than impede human rights, encourage frank discussions on the possibilities and failures of religious belief and practice. Human rights dialogue must mirror the universalism of human rights.

Human rights models that affirm religious traditions incorporate several important aspects of discourse found in the theories of Gadamer and Habermas. In taking seriously the persistence of religious belief in forming moral values, including human rights, any conversation about human rights must welcome religious belief and religious language. As Gadamer indicates, religious beliefs constitute part of tradition and affect the view of one's horizon. Participants in conversation cannot simply leave their religious beliefs behind, even though they can be understood differently or even modified through dialogue over time. Conversations about religion thus should not serve as mere platforms for religious apology but instead become the means by which we view religious belief critically. The goal of conversation is not blind acceptance, but genuine understanding.

If we are, as Taylor suggests, to understand our partners in conversation as agents with self-understanding, then we must allow them to speak for themselves as persons with histories, ideas, and reasons.

Engaging in conversation with Islamic scholars on human rights involves both accepting their humanity and attempting to understand the shared subject matter of human rights from different perspectives. This does not require that we adopt their views on Islam or on human rights but that we willingly undertake the effort to understand these subject matters from new vantage points.

# —2—

# Maududi, Qutb, and Soroush

## *Humanity and History*

If in conversation we wish to seek, as Gadamer describes, a "fusion of horizons," we must understand each other as people who have reasons for thinking as we do. We must accept each other first and foremost as people who come from backgrounds with unique histories and traditions. We must see the other as having a human face. Humanizing the authors of foreign ideas minimizes the objectification that prevents genuine dialogue from occurring.

Although one can certainly read the works of Islamic religious scholars without knowledge of their individual histories or of the environments in which they write, awareness of their backgrounds and the issues of their times often results in a more profound reading of their texts. Situating the personal biographies of Maududi, Qutb, and Soroush within the larger context of politics, economics, and society reminds us of their very human concerns. Because they write to address problems facing Muslims, a grasp of relevant political, economic, and social crises helps to elucidate why they choose to write about specific topics and offer particular recommendations.

The writings of these contemporary Islamic thinkers concerning human rights draw implicitly on the history of Islamic thought and politics.[1] The promise of human rights arises in large part due to the understanding of historical circumstance that leads up to contemporary events. Comprehension of the ways in which the past affects the present enables a richer, more fruitful discussion by introducing events, figures, and themes that become the subject matters for debate and, eventually, policy. Moreover, an effort to understand the personal and historical circumstances that compose the background of global encounters enables people to enter into human rights dialogue with some awareness of cultural and political legacies and burdens.[2]

Although they may not explicitly refer to specific political events or figures that influenced their writings on human rights, Maududi, Qutb, and Soroush inherit a religious tradition that has been inextricably intertwined with politics since its founding days. This, of course, is not to say that all political history in Islamic states was sanctioned by religious norms. On the contrary, as with many political entities, rulers of Islamic states often exploited religious thought as merely a means to power. One could argue that much of Islamic history consists of a tension, oftentimes great and occasionally nonexistent, between the political and the religious. Especially in the last century, religious thought often followed the demands of modernity. Historical events, particularly as they related to colonialism, often inspired creative theological interpretations of Islam.[3] These new theologies, although grounded in traditional sources, varied widely in their responses to colonial threats. The remainder of this chapter aims to provide a basic orientation to the religious, biographical, and historical contexts of Maududi, Qutb, and Soroush. I focus primarily on the events and ideas that most directly affected these thinkers. Therefore, twentieth-century India/Pakistan, Egypt, and Iran receive the most attention, even as numerous other developments unfolded in those countries and around the world.

## SUNNI AND SHI‘I

The Sunni Islamic revival in the twentieth century is often credited to Maududi and Qutb, and contemporary theological reform within the Shi‘i country of Iran is associated with Soroush. Although the labels of Sunni and Shi‘i are often used to differentiate Muslims, the differences between the two sects concern mainly the issue of the historical leadership of the Muslim community, the *umma*. With regard to basic theological, ritualistic, or ethical practices, the differences between Sunnism and Shi‘ism can appear imperceptible. Nonetheless, the rift between Sunni and Shi‘i has translated over centuries into differences in political and religious emphases. Because the ideas of Maududi, Qutb, and Soroush on human rights do not directly address the issues of historical leadership in Islam, their identification with the two sects emerges obliquely. Stresses in political vocabulary and different relationships with the idea of the caliphate, however, point to subtle distinctions underlying their writings on human rights.

Beginning with basic, universally accepted norms within Islam, one cannot help but notice that four of the five "pillars" of Islam involve the formation of community. These practices date back to the Prophet Muhammad himself, whom the followers of Islam strive to emulate. With the exception of one's personal witnessing (*shahada*) of God and Muhammad, the remaining four pillars of prayer (*salat*), almsgiving (*zakat*), fasting (*sawm*), and pilgrimage (*hajj*) take place with other members of the Muslim community.[4] One might even argue that *shahada,* although performed as an individual, is nonetheless a communal act in that it serves as the entry point into the religious community. Islam is a tradition that in its spirit takes seriously the value of group identity, an essential political value.

The ritual inclusion of Muslims into a singular *umma,* however, belies the historical rifts that have occurred between Muslims. The separation of Muslims into separate sects took place with the death of Muhammad (570–632[5]), the founding prophet of Islam. The majority of Muslims after Muhammad's death believed that the Prophet had not designated a successor and thus had left it up to the living community to determine the next leader. These Muslims, the Sunnis, named after the *sunna* (tradition) of the Prophet, support the tradition of Islam over specific Muslim individuals. The fact that the Prophet did not leave behind a son, but rather close relatives and friends, made the decision concerning the succession of the Prophet a contentious one.

The Shi'i followers of Islam, who make up a minority of Muslims, believe that Muhammad's cousin and son-in-law (married to the Prophet's daughter, Fatimah), 'Ali, was his rightful successor. The Shi'i, so named for creating a following of 'Ali, believe that his line, the only one leading directly from the Prophet, was destined to lead the *umma* even prior to the death of Muhammad. The Prophet reportedly indicated that 'Ali would succeed him following his last pilgrimage to Mecca with the fateful words: "He for whom I was the master, should hence have 'Ali as his master."[6] The Shi'i argue that God would not have left the leadership of the *umma* undecided and reason that the man who was most intimate with the practices and life of the Prophet should logically be the next successor.

The fierce commitment of the Shi'i to 'Ali gradually developed into "the widest possible implications of such a loyalty . . . implications for justice not merely in the soldiers' cause but in all fields . . . implications also for the personal devotional life, for metaphysics, and for the whole range of Islamic concerns." Along the same lines, the loyalty of the Sunni to the community had its "pervasive implications, gradually worked out in a long dialog among the Sunni Muslims."[7] The growth and influence of these separate subcultures within Islam may be traced from the seventh century to the present day.[8]

The differences between the Sunni and Shi'i after the death of the Prophet reverberate in the differences of political and religious vocabulary that followed in the centuries thereafter.[9] For the Sunni, revealing key terms include *khilafa, ijma,* and *bay'ah. Khilafa* refers to the majority-chosen caliph, Abu Bakr, a companion of the Prophet and his father-in-law. *Ijma,* or consensus, also plays an important role in the history of the Sunni. A consensus of the elite members of the *umma* chose Muhammad's companion Abu Bakr instead of 'Ali to succeed the Prophet. The term *bay'ah,* which literally means the clasping of hands, represents an oath of loyalty taken by the electors to their caliph.

For the Shi'i, the political and religious vocabulary that best represents their beliefs on the governance of the *umma* includes terms such as *imamah*, *wilayah*, and *ismah*. The *imamah* refers to the divinely chosen leadership of the *umma* and is distinguished from the human-elected caliph. It suggests more specifically the notion that God would not leave the *umma* without a leader following the death of Muhammad. God, according to the Shi'i, must have already chosen a leader, namely 'Ali, to lead the community. *Wilayah,* closely related to the idea of the *imamah*, refers to the custodianship of the divinely chosen leader over Muslims. The Prophet and those closest to him, particularly his relatives, possessed the intellectual and emotional virtue, or *ismah*, that God requires of the leaders of the Muslim community. 'Ali and his descendants, for the Shi'i, are believed to possess *ismah,* a quality that only God determines.

The differences in stress between the Sunni and the Shi'i, however significant, do not occur over fundamental tenets of Islam. Questions concerning the nature of God, the humanness of Muhammad, and the basic duties of the Muslim are not debated in the way that Christian theologians have argued over competing notions of the Trinitarian God, the divine-human nature of Jesus, and ritual practice. Indeed, in examining the texts of Maududi, Qutb, and Soroush, it is often difficult to trace their ideas about human rights to Sunni or Shi'i Islam. Nonetheless, the differences between the Sunni and the Shi'i have over time "degenerated from a quarrel about the Prophet's successorship into a ritual, theological and legal rift which can, at least obliquely, affect certain basic beliefs and attitudes."[10]

## WESTERN COLONIAL INFLUENCE

In the modern era, the time frame this study deals with most directly, some concerns affect both Sunni and Shi'i Muslims, and others affect one sect more than the other. The rise in social and economic power of industrial Europe in the nineteenth century, manifest especially in the phenomenon of colonialism, left an indelible mark on the culture, politics, and economy of nations with large Muslim populations, both Sunni and Shi'i. For Maududi, Qutb, and Soroush, this period would shape the worlds into which they were born and which they would later try to transform.

The rapid advances in the technological culture of Europe that changed countries from agrarian to industrial not only propelled European nations to world dominance but also affected their worldview. This era, which historian Marshall Hodgson named the "Great Western Transmutation," produced a "technical spirit" that "both Westerners and Muslims were to call 'materialistic.'" The technical superiority of Europe combined with its materialistic spirit translated, for many Muslims of the era, into the tyranny of colonialism. Independent Islamic leadership was not tolerated in any of the Muslim territories where European colonizers reigned. The British, Dutch, and French dominated Muslims living in lands as disparate as India, Java and Sumatra, Persia, Palestine, and Algiers. Taking advantage of regional skirmishes, often intra-Muslim, European colonizers entered into agreements with local leaders and, ultimately, removed them from power. European nations also asserted their political and economic influence by insisting that local governments assume European legal standards of law and order. When a local government failed to do so, Europeans intervened not merely to establish rules of extraterritoriality but also to assert the superiority of European jurisdiction over local jurisdiction, even in so-called sovereign territories.[11]

In Persia the British initially sided with the weak Qajar monarchy against the Russian tsar, but the British went on eventually to dominate parts of Iran as Russia became distracted by the troubles of the Bolshevik revolution. In Algeria, attempts made by Muslims to claim independence from the French even by following French law were violently put to rest.[12] The vast Ottoman Empire, extending from northwest Africa into Chinese-controlled Turkistan, was eventually, and rather randomly, carved up into territories governed by the Russians, French, and British. This practice of delineating territories and controlling local rule regardless of language, ethnicity, or culture was to be found not only in the Ottoman Empire and the Middle East but also in Persia and India.

Initial attempts at colonization by the Europeans were met with some resistance by the populace, particularly against local leaders who were thought complicit in their behavior with the Europeans. Those who did not fare as well under colonial rule found "a new appreciation for the tradition of Islamic reform" that had been rising in the previous century.[13] This new appreciation expressed itself in a range of Islamic thought, including the reformist theology of Muhammad 'Abduh (1849–1905) in Egypt, puritanical Wahhabism in the Arabic peninsula, Jamal al-Din al-Afghani's (1839–1897) reformist philosophy in Persia, and a militant and exclusivist form of Islam found in India. In Bengal, a mixture of violent and class-based Islam took hold, with Bengali peasants attacking landlords, both Muslim and Hindu, put in place by the British government.

This period of rebellion was followed temporarily in the late nineteenth century by an era in which resistance "of any kind was for a time at a minimum; acceptance of Western leadership and control, and even outright trust of Western good intentions, were at a maximum."[14] During this period, European-style schools, typically run by Christian missionaries, educated the children of the wealthy and the cultural elite. This young generation of colonized peoples learned English and French, studied European history, and imitated Continental mannerisms.[15] Major European-style institutions, from police and military forces to financial and commercial practices, became more firmly established. This period of "stabilization," however, was unable to soothe the underlying tensions that would lead to a rise of nationalism against imperialism.

The maintenance of class division among the local populations and the lack of capital investments back into the territories contributed to the growing animosity of colonized Muslims against their colonizers.[16] The vast majority of people in colonized lands remained poor and unprepared to thrive in European empires, in large part because colonizers failed to invest whatever capital they gained from their ventures back into the colonies.[17] Hence, the kind of infrastructure required for the colonies to "catch up" to their European counterparts never materialized. Roads, railways, and commercial crops, for example, were never developed enough to help colonized territories compete with European states. Even though the situation in Persia was not as bleak as in North Africa and the Levant, the pressure to hand over oil and tobacco to foreign interests, together with the reckless spending of the shah, promised only devastating consequences for the people. The growing material divide and resulting psychological frustration would lead to the rise in nationalism seen toward the beginning of the twentieth century.

The rise in "nationalism" among colonized Muslims followed complex and blurry lines. The borders drawn by their colonizers did not follow divisions among previous empires, native tongues, religion, or ethnicity. Given the mixture of peoples in the wide geographic region ranging from the western shores of North Africa to the westernmost regions of China, Muslims, as well as Christians and Jews, who lived under colonial rule identified themselves not in terms of nation-state but instead in multiple categories—what national allegiance, for example, would an Arabic-speaking, ethnically Persian, Shi'i Muslim in Ottoman Egypt bear? An attempt to create a pan-Islamic caliphate by an eschatological Madhist movement in the Sudan briefly sparked the hope that such questions would no longer be necessary, but it quickly died out and was subsumed under the massive division and colonization of African lands completed at the turn of the century.

This period directly precedes and overlaps with the lives of Maududi, Qutb, and Soroush. The colonial legacy of the Great Western Transmutation shaped the environments of the countries in which these men lived. The significant political, cultural, and economic changes that happened over the course of their lives would have a profound impact on their understanding of Islam and human rights.

## ABUL A'LA MAUDUDI (1903–1979): INDIA AND PAKISTAN

Maududi witnessed a dramatic transformation of his homeland over the course of his lifetime. The part of colonized India where Maududi was born would at the time of his death lie within the fledgling independent nation of Pakistan. Raised in a Muslim middle-class family in Hyderabad, India, where his father was a lawyer, Maududi studied at a madrasa that combined Muslim and Western-style education. He then attended a secular college until the death of his father prevented him from completing his studies. Despite the premature end of his formal schooling, Maududi had by this point already acquired enough knowledge of Arabic, Persian, English, and Urdu, as well as the intellectual skills, to enable him to continue his studies. Maududi was never formally trained in Islamic law and theology, but he eventually developed a reputation ranking him among the most influential of the ulama. His ideas concerning Islam and politics, in fact, would profoundly affect the writings of Qutb.

Maududi's involvement in the political life of India began when he was a young man. He first established his reputation in his late teens and early twenties as a writer and editor of Muslim newspapers, including *Muslim* and *Al-Jamiyat.* Also around this time, he became involved in political organizations that aimed to overthrow decades of British rule in India.

In the early 1800s the British had cast aside the Muslim rule of the Timurid dynasty, based in Delhi, in favor of a ruling class headed by the British and administered by Hindus. Over the next several decades, the British, aided by a new class of loyal Hindus, removed many of the remaining ruling Muslim families from positions of power. The obvious decline of Muslim power translated for some Muslims, such as Sayyid Ahmad Khan (1817–1898), into a revisioning of Muslim theology that took into account the demands of the dominant British culture. Stressing the "spirit" of the Qur'an, Khan upheld the virtues of individual freedom, the goods of prosperity, and the value of scientific inquiry. Although classically trained ulama found Khan's interpretation of Islam unacceptable, the larger Muslim population embraced the practicality of his theology for the situation in which they found themselves. Khan's theology enabled Indian Muslims to establish themselves as part of the new political and economic system and yet remain good Muslims. His assimilationist views, however, would be challenged with the rise in nationalist feeling at the start of the twentieth century.

As with the people of other territories under British colonial rule, Indians during World War I witnessed invigorated feelings of nationalism. The British had promised the Indians self-rule in exchange for their cooperation during the war. Indians were even sent to fight on behalf of the British army and navy, and the subcontinent itself housed war industries. At the end of the war, however, the British determined that self-rule for the large and unwieldy territory would not be feasible and withdrew their initial promise of independence. Home rule became the cause that Mohandas Gandhi would take up, guided by his philosophy of *satyagraha*, or truth-force. Incorporating ideas from world religions and Western philosophy, Gandhi developed nonviolent strategies for combating the injustices of colonialism.

Many Indian Muslims were initially wary of joining Gandhi's movement because they still hoped for a pan-Islamism under an Ottoman caliphate. At the very least, the Indian Muslim population wanted to see the British offer the Turks a peace treaty that would enable them to maintain leadership of the world *umma.* Not until 1920, when the Indian National Congress, the party led by Gandhi, demanded this recognition of Turkey did Muslims consider Gandhi an ally and support his movement for home rule. Aided by the leadership of Muhammad 'Ali Jinnah (1876–1948), Gandhi was able to garner Muslim support for the independence movement. The end of the caliphate in Ottoman Turkey in 1924, which dashed many Indian Muslims' hopes for an international *umma* led by the sultan, further expedited the alliance between Muslims and the Congress party.

Undoubtedly moved by the Indian independence movement under the leadership of Gandhi, and yet aware of the complexities that would arise out of this emancipation and the possibility of a Muslim *umma,* Maududi offered a perspective on Islam and politics different from that of other Islamic thinkers who lived in Muslim-majority societies. Whereas Muslims in the Middle East formed the majority population of those under colonial rule, the Muslims in India were a minority population with no designated territory. Moreover, British colonialism on the subcontinent lasted longer and was more pervasive than that found elsewhere. The Muslims of India prior to partition experienced colonialism and nationalism on a scale quite apart from Muslims around the Mediterranean and in Persia.[18] Although the colonial experience was similar in the broad respect that the local culture and peoples were subjected to foreign rule, the experience of Muslims in India was distinctive. Maududi's writings would reflect this unique insight into the political life of Muslims in India and, later, Pakistan.

Maintaining one foot in politics and one foot in scholarship, Maududi had kept abreast of the anticolonial movement garnering strength in the 1920s and commented on the role that Indian Muslims might have on an independent subcontinent. As editor of *Tarjuman al-Qur'an* (*Exegesis of the Qur'an*), Maududi continued, as he would for the remainder of his life, to publish essays and opinion pieces on the life of Muslims in India (and later, Pakistan), the West, and Islam. He moved from Hyderabad to Punjab to establish with Muhammad Iqbal (1877–1938) an Islamic center where Muslim scholars could meet, study, and write.

Other Indian Muslim scholars contemporaneous with Maududi included Abul Kalam Azad (1888–1958), who with Jinnah had developed new ways of incorporating Islam into Gandhi's vision. They focused on the freedom and justice of home rule and the universal Qur'anic message of social justice. Islam commanded that Muslims, regardless of their geographic or historical circumstance, fight for freedom and justice. This vision of Hindu–Muslim harmony, however, would quickly deteriorate. Although the majority of Muslims at this time favored such messages of universal justice, a growing minority of Muslims argued for the uniqueness of Islam and the need for a separate Muslim territory. By 1940 the Muslim League, led by Jinnah, had articulated a position in favor of the creation of Pakistan, a separate Muslim majority state.

Aided in large part by the Muslim League and the influence of thinkers such as Iqbal, Muslim separatists were able to gain a stronger political hold with the outbreak of World War II. Because members of the Congress Party, including Gandhi, were interned by the British during the war for fear of losing much-needed Hindu loyalty, the Muslim League was able to strengthen and maintain its position for partition. The end of the war coincided with a massive famine in Bengal and the outbreak of massacres, both of which indicated that British rule in India was no longer effective. With the realization that they had to withdraw from India, the British sent Viscount Mountbatten to negotiate independence and partition.

In the debate over whether Muslims should establish their own state, separate from a Hindu India, Maududi initially argued against such a creation and asserted that the establishment of a political Muslim state defined by borders violated the idea of the universal *umma.*[19] Citizenship and national borders, which would characterize the new Muslim state, contradicted the notion that Muslims should not be separated from one another by these temporal boundaries. In this milieu, Maududi founded the organization Jama'at-i Islami.[20] From its founding in 1941 until 1972, Maududi played a leadership role in the organization, which aimed to strengthen the ties among Muslims throughout the world. The Jama'at for its first few years worked actively to prevent the partition, but once partition became inevitable, it established offices in both Pakistan and India.

As Maududi may have predicted, the creation of Pakistan resulted in a massive migration of Hindus out of and Muslims into the region. In addition, the partition effectively eliminated the possibility for a Sikh homeland. During August and September 1947, after the peaceful transfer of power and land to Pakistan, violence ensued. Between two hundred thousand and five hundred thousand Muslim men, women, and children trying to cross the border into Pakistan were murdered, presumably by Indian nationalists who opposed the partition. Massacres on a smaller scale occurred on the other side of the partition.

After the partition, Maududi moved to Pakistan, where he worked to make Pakistan a state founded on Islamic principles. He often opposed the Pakistani government, particularly with regard to its pro-Western policies, and offered numerous commentaries as to how Pakistan should develop as an Islamic nation. Among his prolific writings, he published works on such topics as just war, human rights, and legal theory. Though not formally a member of the ulama, Maududi at times served as their unofficial spokesperson and at other times disagreed publicly with them, especially on the participation of women in politics and the issue of *ijtihad* (innovative legal interpretation), both of which he favored so long as they were confined within the parameters of the *shari'a* (Islamic law).[21]

Maududi continued to write during the last decades of his life, which was marked alternatively by condemnation from the Pakistani government, including a death sentence that was later commuted, and adoration from his followers abroad, whom he met during his extensive travels. Maududi's last visit abroad was to the United States, where he sought medical treatment for his ailing health. He passed away in 1979.

## SAYYID QUTB (1906–1966): EGYPT

As with Maududi's India, the Egypt in which Qutb grew up changed dramatically over the course of his lifetime. Politically and intellectually, Egypt was an epicenter of change and struggle during the first half of the twentieth century.[22] It comes as no surprise that Qutb, arguably the "most significant thinker of Islamic resurgence in the modern Arab world," would have observed and participated in this dynamic environment.[23] For more than thirty-four years, the Egyptian Qutb would produce a prolific amount of scholarship on a range of topics, including Islamic politics, economics, the West, Qur'anic interpretation, and even literary criticism. His writings on human rights come to fruition most notably toward the end of his career in such texts as *Social Justice in Islam* (1948), *The Battle between Islam and Capitalism* (1950), and *Milestones* (1964). Like Maududi, Qutb was not formally trained in Islamic law or theology, but his knowledge and influence allowed him to become a formidable religious scholar.

Qutb was not born into Egypt's intellectual or religious class but rather into a peasant family in a rural village outside of Cairo, and he was educated in secular schools. In his autobiography, *Tifl min al-Qaryah* (*A Child from the Village*), Qutb shares his early observations of the unjust treatment of the poor by village leaders, including the sheik. Empathy for the poor and wariness of hypocritical religious believers appear repeatedly as themes in his writings on social justice. As a teenager, Qutb left for Cairo to further his education and established there a reputation as a poet and literary critic. Even as he gradually joined the ranks of prominent Muslim intellectuals and political activists, his writings throughout his career continued to reflect his personal ties to the poor.

Prior to writing *Social Justice in Islam,* Qutb extensively studied the literature and philosophy of Western thinkers. Influenced by Taha Hussein (1889–1973), a legendary scholar and educator who advocated Western-style modernization for Egypt, Qutb began to examine closely the relationship between culture and imperialism. Colonialism was not merely an economic and political phenomenon but also, and most insidiously, a cultural one. In the Egypt into which Qutb was born, the stage had been set by a number of remarkable scholars and activists who debated whether Islam should be the force behind political, economic, and social change.

In Egypt the demise of colonialism and the rise of nationalism took place alongside a revival of Islam.[24] Egyptian Muslims, with the aid of well-educated Syrian Christians, restored the tarnished image of the Arabic language and, with it, of Islamic history. Such scholars as ‘Abduh revitalized Islam in Egypt by developing a Sunni theology on the basis of the writings of thinkers such as Muhammad al-Ghazali (1058–1111) and the early rationalist school of the Mut‘azila but adapted to the demands of the modern times.[25] Inspired personally by the teachings of the Persian scholar Afghani, who went on to encourage anticolonial, democratic movements in his own homeland, ‘Abduh sought to propel Egyptians into modernity.[26] He fought against *taqlid,* or “blind imitation” and “uncritical faith” in Islamic legal precedent, which he believed prevented Egypt from adapting to the requirements of the present age.[27] Rather than imitate outdated jurisprudence, ‘Abduh asserted the need to rely on both rational capacities and faith to guide Muslims in this new era. ‘Abduh, who “consistently sought to remain within the traditionally Sunni mainstream, argued for harmony between sound reason and revelation, which he thought could never stand in conflict.”[28]

‘Abduh’s reformist theology proved but one of the many ways in which Islam could be revived. His most prominent student, the Syrian Rashid Rida (1865–1935), moved gradually away from the use of rationalism in Islam to a Wahhabist defense of the unchanging perfection of Islam.[29] Unable to maintain the balance required for a careful reformation of Islamic jurisprudence, Rida eventually advocated “strict obedience to the Qur’an and Hadith, and rejection of all that could be regarded as illegitimate innovations.”[30] The influence of Wahhabist thought continued to expand well into the twentieth century.

The *Salafiyyah* movement, also born out of ‘Abduh’s thought, was, like Wahhabism, extremely traditional and very suspicious of local interpretations of Islam and Sufism. Named after the *salaf,* or the first three generations of Muslims, this movement attempted to enforce strict adherence to *shari‘a.* Members of the *Salafiyyah* movement likewise tried to incorporate a vision of an earlier, purer version of Islam into modern times. They advocated above all a conservative, patriarchal lifestyle that revolved around religious worship.

In stark contrast to the ethics of the Wahhabi and *Salafiyyah,* ‘Abduh’s student Qasim Amin (1863–1908) articulated a vision of radical equality between men and women that far surpassed the imagination of the Muslim public. Amin perceived the Arab, Muslim culture as inferior to the West, proved by unjust differences in status between the sexes. Although the majority of Egyptians found Amin's thought blasphemous, several women heeded his message. They stopped wearing the veil and took jobs in what were traditionally male occupations. The diversity of thought that emerged from 'Abduh was part of a larger attempt to define the culture of a colonized population.

'Abduh's reformist thought, pro-independence, pro-Arab, and pro-Muslim, represented one strand of nationalism that arose out of the experience of colonies during World War I. Egypt was at the time technically under British rule, but Arabs sympathized, at least initially, more with the Muslims of the Ottoman Empire. The quashing of Arab independence movements by the Committee of Union and Progress in other parts of the Ottoman Empire, however, led pro-Arab activists to change their allegiances to the British in exchange for eventual Arab independence. Egyptian Arabs thus fought with the British against Turkish Ottomans in World War I in anticipation of their emancipation. Unfortunately, when the Europeans won the war, they secretly rearranged and divided the Middle East region into spheres of influence, instead of giving their colonies outright self-determination as promised. Even if they were no longer in direct control of these areas, the British, French, and Italians dominated the political and economic policies of the region. Predictably, Arabs staged open revolts and resistance movements against their European occupiers. Responding also to the frustration of families back home that rallied for the return of their troops, the British soon removed themselves from a worsening political climate. These movements for independence in the 1920s and 1930s eventually led to a series of treaties that increased local control but also allowed the European countries to exploit natural resources, the Suez Canal, and valuable lands.

These events and the political engagement of Muslim activists such as 'Abduh had a profound impact on Qutb. Although Qutb in his early years found the pro-Western ideas of Hussein appealing, he would later find the perspectives of the *Salafiyyah* truer to the experiences of Egyptians and to his own personal observations. During a visit to the United States in the late 1940s, for instance, Qutb became convinced of the immorality of the West, especially in its loose sexual mores, and returned determined not to allow Western cultural influence to sully what was left of Islam in Egypt. Qutb doubted the notion, touted by several Muslim intellectuals, that adopting Western culture would be the best means toward modernization. Although the United States and Western Europe were far more advanced than Egypt technologically, they suffered morally. In Qutb's opinion, imitating Western culture would come at too great a moral cost.

On his return from the United States, Qutb formalized his association with the Ikhwan, or the Muslim Brotherhood, founded by Hasan al-Banna (1906–1949). Convinced that the Qur'an and early Islamic precepts would guide Egypt out of the hands of corrupting Western influences, Qutb found much sympathy in the membership of the Ikhwan. The Muslim Brotherhood, in its uncompromising stance against the West and its approval of violence as a means to desired ends, posed a threat to the Egyptian government, which did not always formulate policies to the approval of the brotherhood. The Egyptian government twice outlawed membership in the brotherhood and tortured and jailed its members, including Qutb. From the mid-1950s until his death a decade later, Qutb spent most of his life in prison, completing his thirty-volume Qur'anic exegesis, *In the Shade of the Qur'an.* Under the government of Jamal Abdul Nasser, Qutb was convicted of treason and hanged in 1966.

## ABDOLKARIM SOROUSH (1945–PRESENT): PERSIA AND IRAN

By the time of Abdolkarim Soroush's birth, colonial rule was formally ending in much of the world. Egypt had been declared an independent nation in 1922, and India and Pakistan would follow in 1947. Western colonialism, economically and culturally, had not been thrust on Persia (officially named Iran in 1935) in the same way that it had been for Egypt or India, however.[31] Somewhat geographically distanced from the events around the Mediterranean and protected by formidable topography, the Persians were able to escape some of the more brutal aspects of colonialism, but were still close enough to enable travel and investment between Persians and Europeans. Unfortunately for the Persians, corrupt rule made such transactions far more profitable for the Europeans than for themselves.

In part to finance his extravagant trips to Europe, Naser-al-Din Shah, who reigned from 1848 to 1896, proposed, in the 1870s, opening up the Persian economy to further investment by European companies. In his most notorious action, he permitted the British Imperial Tobacco Corporation to develop and maintain a vertical monopoly of the tobacco industry in Persia for fifty years in exchange for 25 percent of the profits and an annual rent.[32] At around the same time, the shah invited Afghani to Persia, not realizing the extent to which he would inspire the people to rise up against colonial influence. Afghani advocated religious and political reforms that would enable Muslims to form a pan-Islamic movement to stand up to Western powers. Persuading the Persians of a slippery slope to eventual domination, Afghani led the people in a massive boycott against the tobacco industry. With the help of the ulama, who issued a fatwa against the use of tobacco products, Afghani led a countrywide effort to make tobacco so unprofitable that the shah and the British were forced to concede the monopoly. The "Tobacco Rebellion" of 1891–1892, mythologized in Iranian national history, would foreshadow the importance of the ulama in forming public political opinion.

The decades leading up to World War I consisted of intermittent strides toward nationalism spurred on each time by the shah's attempts to take out massive loans from the British or the Russians. Opposed to foreign indebtedness, the public, at times led by the more democratic members of the *majlis* (parliament), managed to keep some control of their national economy. During the war, however, the British and the Russians took over parts of Persia to block German influence coming from southeastern provinces. As a revolution back home required Russia to remove itself from Persia, the British remained the sole foreign influence in Persia at the end of World War I. During this time, nationalistic movements in Persia were in full swing. Reza Khan, a decisive military and political leader, ended the Qajar dynasty and in 1926 crowned himself the new shah of Persia.[33]

In contrast to Turkey's Mustafa Kemal, who zealously adopted all things Western, Reza Shah approached the adoption of Western trends slightly more cautiously and strengthened or revived Persian ones. For example, although Persians carried out some modern changes associated with the West, they also implemented a new Persian calendar to replace the Western Gregorian one.[34] Specific influences from the West that crept into Persian society included communist theories from Russia and cultural trends from Europe. Feminism, state factories, and Western-style dress, for example, were characteristic of this era. Though he maintained his throne, Reza Shah was perceived very poorly by oppressed rural Iranians and dismissed by the elite. With the British and Soviets invading Iran to use it as a bulwark against Hitler in the USSR, World War II was to prove Reza Shah's rule untenable, and thus he stepped down from power. His son, Mohammad-Reza Pahlavi, assumed the crown in 1941.

Mohammad-Reza Shah had ruled for four years by the time Soroush entered the world, and he continued to reign well into Soroush's adulthood. Soroush, born into a working-class family in Tehran, attended the highly regarded Alavi High School, whose founders adopted an educational philosophy that embraced both the modern sciences and religious teaching. During this period, Soroush briefly spent time with groups that compared Shi'i Islam to the Baha'i religion and that identified themselves with a particular sect of Sunnism or Shi'ism. Indicative of his scholarly nature, he would leave these organizations because he found their sectarianism intellectually unsound. Although he no longer participated in these groups, he continued to explore the beliefs of different religious faiths and to investigate rigorously their various claims. His early experiences, as well as his precocious interest in poetry, have affected his philosophical and theological writings to the present day.[35]

In the years following World War II, the struggle for oil highlighted the continuing competition between foreign power and national interest in Iran. An experienced nationalist politician, Mohammad Mossadeq (1882–1967), was elected prime minister in 1951 and led a movement to nationalize the oil industry, which to this point had been blatantly exploited by the British. The British, fully aware of the negative impact the loss of Iranian oil would have on their economy, considered employing military force to coerce the Iranians into giving up their efforts to control their own oil. Prime Minister Clement Attlee, however, reasoned that British use of the military to require a nation to give up its own resources at absurdly low prices did not constitute justifiable use of force. Therefore, the British, after seeking advice from the United Nations and the support of the newest superpower, the United States, allowed Iran to take control of its own oil. This move ostensibly seemed to help the Iranians self-administer and profit from their natural resources. Because Britain and the United States purchased most of Iran's oil, however, they were able to use their buying power to demand artificially low oil prices, thereby causing a financial crisis in Iran. In 1953 the shah, with the assistance of a coup orchestrated by the U.S. Central Intelligence Agency, removed Mossadeq as prime minister. In exchange for the shah's cooperation, the British and the Americans agreed to settle the dispute over oil. For the United States and Britain, this agreement meant that they now had a strategic hold in containing communist influence from the Soviet Union. The involvement of the Central Intelligence Agency in maintaining the shah was to last nearly three decades, until the Islamic Revolution in 1979.[36]

These events unfolded as Soroush entered the University of Tehran to study pharmacy and, privately, to pursue Islamic philosophy. During the mid-1960s, his acquaintance with the rise of the anti-imperial guerrilla group Mojahedin-e Khalq ("The People's Holy Warriors") led him to explore Marxism and to ponder the relationship between religion and politics. Soroush's interest in the relationship between religion and politics was further reinforced by the lectures of Professor Ali Shari'ati

(1933–1977), who attracted a great number of activist students. When he left for England to continue his graduate work, Soroush added to his breadth of intellectual interests the history and philosophy of science. In his graduate program of study, Soroush acquainted himself with Western philosophers, ranging from Kant and Hume to Gödel and Kuhn, who would also influence his later theology and epistemology.

As Soroush was continuing his studies in Europe, discontent back in his home country began to reach a fever pitch. Frustrated by decades of ineffectual reform, soaring inflation, indiscriminate military use against the people, and a gross divide between the wealthy and the poor, the people of Iran under the leadership of an exiled religious leader began to demonstrate. In January 1978, students in the holy city of Qom rallied for the return of the Ayatollah Khomeini from Najaf. In response, the shah ordered the police to fire on them, and several students were killed. This incident set off a series of protests throughout the country, with thousands more citizens killed by the state army. These events made clear that the shah could no longer maintain his position in Iran. Khomeini returned to Iran in 1979 to lead the Islamic Republic. He blamed the United States for the problems that befell Iran under the shah, and several of his loyal followers reacted by attacking the American Embassy and holding fifty-two Americans hostage until President Jimmy Carter left office in 1981. Over the next decades, Iran's government, which initially promised nationalism and reform, would take on a decidedly traditionalist and conservative tone, much to the dismay of its revolutionaries.

In September 1979, following the Islamic Revolution, Soroush returned to Iran. He chaired the Department of Islamic Culture at Tehran's Teachers' College and sat on the Advisory Council of the Cultural Revolution, a position from which he later resigned. His increasingly critical stance toward the Iranian government, barely disguised in his academic writings, led to his tenuous relationship with the current clerical order. Soroush has expressed his disappointment with leaders of the revolution who became hard-line reactionaries. Since the early 1980s and up to the present day, he has held professorships at several universities, including Harvard, and maintains a position as researcher for the Institute for Cultural Research and Studies in Tehran, where he teaches Islamic philosophy and theology.

## RECOGNIZING THE HORIZONS OF OTHERS: A CONVERSATION BEGINS

This brief history of Muslim politics in the last century provides a backdrop for the thinkers highlighted in this book. These events and the issues that arose undoubtedly affected Maududi, Qutb, and Soroush, who served and continue to serve as "public intellectuals" for their audiences. They participated in the politics of their countries using their scholarly and theological knowledge to provide clarity and guidance to Muslims of their own troubled countries and beyond.

Although these broad strokes of history do not determine the direction of their scholarship, the experience of colonialism and its aftereffects permeate these thinkers' writings. They may not address or mention specific events in their theological essays, but such events cannot be ignored. Maududi and Qutb write at times scathingly about the West because of their direct experience with European imperialists. What they did not experience directly, they witnessed through reports and the scholarship of others. They observed the oppression of their religious communities, the plundering of their ways of life, and the exploitation of natural resources throughout the Muslim world. They also noted, beyond the physical and material damage wrought by colonialism, the psychological and spiritual harms that colonial rule brought on their people. Soroush, born after Maududi and Qutb, also felt the repercussions of British and then American imperialism, this time on Iranian soil. In addition to this history, Soroush refers to the more recent changes in the Iranian government from revolutionary to reactionary. His critical understanding of religion and jurisprudence, democracy, and freedom emerges directly from his observations of Iranian politics. The writings of Maududi, Qutb, and Soroush, as ageless as they are, address contemporary situations. They draw on the Qur'an, *hadith, sunna,* Islamic jurisprudence, and their Sunni and Shi'i traditions to illuminate the events and dilemmas of their times.

The matters that concern Maududi, Qutb, and Soroush extend beyond their geographical and temporal boundaries. Events and encounters on the level of the individual are not necessarily determinative of their thoughts. Nonetheless, their biographies provide some insight into their particular intellectual and spiritual influences, as well as additional perspectives on their scholarship and concerns.

These thinkers, and the historical context that surrounded them, produced the writings analyzed in the following chapters. The extent to which circumstance determined substance was and is debatable. Nonetheless, because these thinkers consciously address the issues of the day, an awareness of the world around them and the lives that they lived helps to convey the meaning their works might have for their audiences.

Recognizing the human faces behind different perspectives plays an essential role in initiating and sustaining a conversation about Islam and human rights. We must accept our interlocutors—just as we assume of ourselves—as possessing self-understanding and having histories that shape individual horizons. To discuss the subject matter of human rights with the hope of coming to some agreement requires that we converse always to honor the humanity of our conversation partners.

# —3—

# Envisioning Islamic Democracies

Although Maududi, Qutb, and Soroush agree that democracy is a human right and that Islam supports democracy, they conceive of Islamic democracies in different ways. Their individual visions of democracy derive from their unique religious, historical, and political views. In entering into conversation with these thinkers about democracy as a human right supported by Islam, we hope to come to an understanding about this subject matter by first accepting their views of democracy as arising out of traditions different from our own. We also bring to this dialogue sensitivity to the historical circumstances that may affect their visions of democracy and Islam.

Keenly aware of the historical contexts in which they write, Maududi, Qutb, and Soroush grapple with the prospect of democracy in Muslim nations that are freshly independent of colonial rule and eager to distinguish themselves from Western culture. The scholars conceive of distinct versions of religious democracy, each of which displays the unique concerns and attitudes that emerge from a particular individual, time, and location. These thinkers draw on intellectual and spiritual resources to develop democratic ideas out of Islamic traditions.

Democracy, defined broadly as a government for which the people assume responsibility, requires not only free and fair elections but also stable supporting institutions.[1] Maududi, Qutb, and Soroush discuss in depth the teachings of Islam with regard to these supporting institutions of democracy, particularly free press and schools. They recognize the importance of selecting a leader by democratic means, but they place an emphasis on the economic stability, intellectual preparedness, and physical well-being of the electorate prior to the establishment of democracy. Maududi, Qutb, and Soroush defend the idea that Muslims need not abandon Islam while in pursuit of democracy.[2] They subscribe to the beneficial coexistence of religion and the democratic process but recommend different strategies for Islamic democracies. Maududi and Qutb spend most of their efforts finding inspiration in the Qur'an, *sunna,* and *hadith* to support democratic ideas and institutions. They present apologetic views of both the Islamic political process and Islamic history and contrast their mollified vision of Islam to a sordidly portrayed West. The West, they believe, falls far short of its purported democratic aims. Soroush also argues that Islam presents a uniquely comprehensive view of democratic government that cares for the spiritual as well as the material needs of its citizens, but unlike Maududi and Qutb, he avoids direct comparisons with the West, although he draws inspiration from Western thinkers. The contrast in attitudes among the three toward the West emerges out of the different selection, interpretation, and application of religious resources toward perceived political, social, and economic conditions.

## ISLAM AS THE "PERFECT" DEMOCRACY

Maududi argues in *Human Rights in Islam* that Islam is a form of democracy, though unlike the kind of democracy found in the West. He considers Islam the "perfect" form of democracy in contrast to the secular political forms found in Europe and North America.[3] In an Islamic democracy, sovereignty lies with God, and the people are his representatives, or caliphs, whereas in Western democracies, sovereignty exists without regard for God.

In his understanding of democracy, Maududi advocates popular rule, though not on the basis of the sovereignty of human beings. Rather, he advocates a democracy on the basis of the sovereignty of God, whose will is carried out by people. The difference between a theocracy and a democracy in Islam, then, is that in a theocracy, only a few religious leaders represent God, whereas in an Islamic democracy, every person can act as a representative of God.[4] All individuals in an Islamic government enjoy the rights accorded to them as caliphs and therefore exist as equals in government.[5]

Although everyone in an Islamic democracy contributes to its rule, government does not become anarchic or despotic in that power exists uncontrollably in the hands of the many or of the few. Rather, participants in such a democracy understand that their decisions must be made in accordance with divine law and as prescribed in revealed scripture. Public opinion in an Islamic democracy would therefore not allow for the flourishing of evil or greed. Maududi believes that an Islamic democracy differs from a Western-style democracy in that citizens of an Islamic democracy consider God's will in making their decisions, whereas Western citizens consider only themselves.[6] Western democracy falls prey to the fallibility of human selfishness and to all its attendant sins.

Despite his claims that Western democracies are spiritually impoverished, Maududi realizes that such governments, particularly those in the United States and Britain, claim moral superiority due to their triumph in the Second World War. Maududi contrasts the moral and material prowess of the Allied powers with those of Japan and Germany as well as with Muslim countries. He claims that the only reason why the governments of the United States, Britain, and the Soviet Union could defeat the Japanese and the Germans was because of their overwhelming material resources, as opposed to their morality. He argues that Germany and Japan were superior in several ways to the Allied nations. Germany, he believes, even held an edge over the Allied forces in its understanding and application of science and technology. Nevertheless, the Allies benefited from larger populations, greater natural resources, and advantageous geographical positioning. The Allied powers won the war only because of their material resources and their desire for power, not because of their moral strength.[7]

Maududi uses the example of the Allies in World War II to demonstrate a principle of comparative moral and physical powers. He develops a mathematical formula to show how a relative lack of material strength can be compensated by a dose of Islamic morals. He argues that Islamic morality makes up for a lack of material strength by a ratio of one to four. That is, Muslims need only a quarter of what non-Muslims possess in material strength because the remainder is made up through superior morality. Moreover, Muslims can improve this ratio even more to their favor if they are able to live the morally exemplary lives of the first Muslims. In such a case, the ratio improves such that Muslims will require only one-tenth of the material goods of the enemy, and the 90 percent deficiency will be made up by Islamic morality. He refers to the Qur'an in support of his claim: "If there be twenty patient and persevering men among you, they will triumph over two hundred adversaries" (8:65).[8] If Muslims practice Islamic morality, they can form a government, if not a world leadership, that no rival can defeat.

Much of Maududi's message concerns the formation of a government that is not merely just but also free of immorality and ungodliness.

In the kind of democracy he envisions, the people would demand that ungodly and immoral behavior be stopped and that virtuous deeds be fostered. Maududi encourages like-minded moral people to work collectively in order to remove morally corrupt persons from positions of power. In this effort, Maududi suggests that Muslims, Christians, and Jews share the same command. He claims that followers of the three Abrahamic traditions share the same objectives. Perhaps, however, more so than with the other Abrahamic religions, Islam's "ultimate purpose" requires that people act cooperatively to establish and preserve a religiously guided society. Muslims should commit themselves solely to God, which entails that they live their lives according to the law of God.[9]

The failure of what Maududi deems an Islamic revolution results from a number of reasons, including ignorance, weak and immoral leadership, and prejudice against Islam. Muslims and non-Muslims alike fail to understand the centrality of establishing a divinely based government in Islam. Too often, leaders of Muslim governments view their role as solely political and fail to appreciate the centrality of religious belief in their lives. They view their role as secular and display no understanding of themselves as leaders within a religious tradition. Correspondingly, Muslims fail to see that the problems plaguing society stem from immoral governance and that citizens have a responsibility to ensure that the leaders of society embody virtue.[10] Maududi chastises Muslims for believing that they are meeting the requirements of Islam simply by carrying out worship rites. Like their leaders, they fail to see the larger picture of Islam and are merely performing religious rituals rather than appreciating its greater vision.

## UNITY AND COLLABORATION

Qutb asserts the uniqueness of Islamic governance, even if it appears similar in several respects to "man-made political systems." Although some superficial similarities may exist between Islam and other forms of governance, Islam requires a unity of secular and sacred, material and spiritual, which the others do not. Islam, in other words, integrates spiritual and bodily needs and recognizes that theological beliefs are inseparable from secular life. Islam both includes and transcends economic justice because its ability to motivate citizens surpasses the level of justice dictated through secular law.[11] Islam's version of justice rests equally on the conscience and the law.

Unlike Soroush and Maududi, Qutb does not mention the term "democracy" explicitly in his writings. Rather, he uses terms often associated with democracy, such as "equality" and "freedom," when writing about governance and just rule. Writing about just rule without mention of the term democracy is Qutb's attempt to distinguish completely Islam from what he terms "Western" political systems. He stresses repeatedly that Islam differs from these other ways of ruling because of the unity of the material and the spiritual in Islam. Western nations, which include the capitalist and Christian United States and European states, as well as communist countries, fail to understand how both material necessities and spiritual fulfillment are required for a truly just government. Capitalism and communism "wrongly stress the material side of humanity over the spiritual, while Christianity wrongly stresses the spiritual side over the material."[12] Islam stands proudly alone in its comprehensive approach to human nature and governance.

Even more so than his contemporaries, Qutb stresses the connection between justice and the material well-being of the people. Equality, the second of three foundations for social justice—the other two being the "absolute freedom of conscience" and "the permanent mutual responsibility of society"—requires that persons possess the basic necessities for life.[13] Although this emphasis on economic justice appears ostensibly similar to the goals of communism and capitalism, given the larger view from which Qutb understands Islam, such emphasis constitutes only one part of the greater whole that is Islam.

Understanding economic justice as the primary goal of Qutb's message overlooks the religious perspective that ultimately determines the importance of economic justice. Economic equality or, more specifically, equality of economic opportunity, plays an important part in Qutb's vision of Islamic governance. Not only does poverty rob citizens of agency and self-worth, but allowing for poverty to exist is a moral offense punishable in the afterlife. Religious law aims to prevent poverty and to end it where it does exist. In so doing, religious law places the burden of responsibility on the state and wealthier members of the community to mitigate the problems of poverty.[14]

Economic discrimination on the basis of race or class violates standards not only of economic justice but also of religious justice.[15] Islamic governments, although they do not insist on an exact equality of wealth, require that persons share their wealth so that equality of opportunity may arise.[16] People have different strengths and capabilities, and, accordingly, they will be rewarded differently. Resulting differences in wealth, however, should not be so great as to interfere with the principle of equal opportunity. All persons, regardless of economic, political, or social standing, should receive opportunities to maximize and capitalize on their talents.[17]

Although Qutb remains concerned about discrimination against the individual, the principle that underlies his understanding of property is that goods generally belong to the community.[18] This principle allows the community to take measures against gross inequities of wealth. Protections against extremes in wealth serve to ensure the health of the community. If any one person severely upsets the balance of wealth in the community, the group suffers. Therefore, some difference in material wealth is permissible and considered natural, but communities should redistribute wealth in order to correct gross imbalances that weaken a fundamental sense of equality among persons.

Communities and the individuals who compose them must use their wealth responsibly. This entails most obviously measures such as *zakat*, or almsgiving religiously mandated to benefit the needy, as well as taxes meant to encourage equality and justice in the community. The collected monies serve two purposes. First, they assist community members in need, and second, they help to preserve the health of the community.[19] By redistributing some wealth, the government controls ill will generated by the excessive wealth imbalance, and it takes back undeserved wealth generated by penury and artificially inflated prices.

Measures taken by the community to redistribute wealth should exist not solely as legislative mandates but also as religious ones. Qutb stresses the role that Islam plays in informing or guiding the conscience with regard to economic equality. Those who possess a great amount of material wealth as well as those who possess undue political influence should by both law and conscience relinquish these advantages to bring balance to the community. Likewise, those who are materially and politically disempowered should by law and by conscience claim or be given goods and power. To claim *zakat* is a right, and to give *zakat* is a reasonable legal obligation, not to be confused with voluntary gifts to charity.[20]

Because these transformations in society arise through Islamic religious law, as well as by civil law, such changes occur as acts of conscience and faith rather than by legal coercion alone. The principle of equality speaks to the conscience of all, regardless of their status in the community. Equality, as an idea and as practiced, emphasizes the unity of human nature spiritually and physically.[21]

In order to achieve the equality found in a just and free society, Qutb asserts the necessity of collaboration, or *shura*, between the rulers and the ruled. Qutb considers collaboration key to establishing equality among people. His reasons for advancing the idea of collaboration and avoiding the term "democracy" lie in his attempt to distinguish Islamic forms of rule from specifically Western forms of government. Hence, although some principles in collaboration may appear similar to those of democracy, collaboration differs from democracy in light of the larger context of Qutb's ideas. His notion of collaboration also differs from

American and European forms of democracy in that collaboration lacks specificity with regard to the structure and procedure of formulating or changing policy. Whereas in the United States and in European countries, governments, at least in theory, have a clear chain of command and detailed channels for creating and changing laws, governments according to Islam have no prescribed way to collaborate with the public. Qutb asserts that "no specific method of administering [*shura*] has even been laid down; its application has been left to the exigencies of individual situations." A defined system of collaboration has not been proved necessary historically, Qutb alleges, because informal consultation meets whatever demand arises. Moreover, the flexibility of an undefined principle of collaboration enables a government to respond to a variety of situations.[22]

In addition to rulers and ruled having a fluid system of collaboration, two elements are necessary for collaboration to succeed. First, rulers must be just; second, the ruled must obey the rulers. If any one of these three pillars is weak, then the other two will fall as well. The just ruler, in Qutb's opinion, should take his lead from the following verses of the Qur'an and the *hadith:*

> "Verily Allah commands justice" (16:92). "And when you judge between the people, you must do so with justice" (4:61). "And when you speak, act justly, even though the matter concerns a relative" (6:153). "And be not driven by hatred of any people to unjust action; to act justly is closer to piety" (5:11). "Verily on the Day of Resurrection he who is dearest of all men to Allah, and he who is nearest to Him will be the just leader; but he who is most hated by Allah on that Day, and he who is most bitterly punished will be the tyrannical leader" (Traditions).

To emphasize the divine command to rulers to govern justly, Qutb adds that a ruler possesses "no extra privileges as regards the law, or as regards wealth; and his family have no such privileges either, beyond those of the generality of Muslims."[23] Rulers have a religious imperative to rule without bias, hatred, or tyranny. Although legal measures may be taken against unjust rulers, Qutb views these divine imperatives as standards by which to rule. As with his earlier explanations regarding the necessity of combining civil, secular rule with religiously informed conscience, Qutb's perspective on just rulers takes both sides into consideration.

Just rulers are limited in the scope of their powers. Qutb draws a line between areas of a citizen's life in which a ruler may interfere and areas in which a ruler may not. "No ruler dare oppress the souls or the bodies of Muslims, nor dare he infringe upon their sanctities, nor touch their wealth. If he upholds the law and sees that religious duties are observed, then he has reached the limit of his powers."[24] Where these lines are drawn between citizens' private lives, where a ruler cannot interfere, and their public lives, where a ruler may interfere, differs considerably from where they are drawn in the United States and in European countries. Nonetheless, that these lines are drawn is significant.[25]

The one area where rulers have the most expansive powers concerns "matters of welfare which pertain to the community." Qutb notes that "while Islam sets a strict limit to the power of a ruler," it gives him the "broadest possible powers" when the health of the community is involved. Because the problems that afflict communities change over time and because solutions to those problems also change, Qutb considers questions of welfare as having "no guiding precedent in existence, and which evolve with the processes of time and with changing conditions."[26] He argues in favor of an individualized approach to dealing with societal problems and reinforces his understanding of ad hoc *shura.*

When deciding on any policy that affects the welfare of the community, Qutb insists, there "must be collaboration between ruler and ruled." He cites the Qur'an to buttress his emphasis on the necessity of collaboration. " 'Take counsel with them in the matter' (3:153). 'And their affair is a matter for collaboration between them' (42:36)." Even with regard to decisions of economic welfare, Qutb does not provide details concerning the administration of finances. He insists that the application of collaboration should be "left to the exigencies of individual situations." The general principle of *shura,* in Qutb's opinion, has been sufficient to meet the demands of the Islamic community. Rather than developing and adhering to a rigid system of solving problems, the Islamic community should feel "content" with and, indeed, see the benefit from "this type of informal counsel." In all cases, collaboration proves advantageous to other forms of rule because it leaves open the option of choosing from any number of systems and methods of governance.[27]

## RELIGIOUS DEMOCRACY

Soroush stands out among Muslim religious scholars for his support of religious democracy rather than an explicitly Islamic democracy. He criticizes secularists' quick dismissal of the possibility of religious democracy, but without asserting the supremacy of Islamic or religious democracy over Western-style democracy. Unlike Maududi and Qutb, he tends to avoid direct comparisons to Western forms of governance. Moreover, Soroush embraces modernity for the positive ways it has changed how we understand the world, especially as it relates to religion. Modernity celebrates a rationality that strives for a universal truth, an end toward which religion also aims. Because universal truth derives from multiple sources of knowledge, Soroush argues, he does not discriminate among religious traditions and readily draws from both Islamic and non-Islamic works.

Soroush defines democracy as "a method of restricting the power of the rulers and rationalizing their deliberations and policies, so that they will be less vulnerable to error and corruption, more open to exhortation, moderation, consultation; and so that violence and revolution will not become necessary." He does not believe that democracy necessarily requires "extreme liberalism" or a separation of religion from government. He tentatively proposes that people can enjoy the freedom of democracies while at the same time acknowledging the existence of God in government. Secular democracies, he acknowledges, do not deprive persons of their right to believe. Nonetheless, secular democracies deal inadequately with the concerns and beliefs of religious persons who constitute part of society. Persons with strong religious convictions should not be expected to hold beliefs internally and suppress them in public life.[28] Religious persons within secular democracies may feel troubled about dismissive attitudes toward questions about God in government. Indeed, secular democracies lack adequate mechanisms required to address such concerns.

Secular democracies' inability to acknowledge religious identity, Soroush argues, contributes to the fear of democracy by some Islamic governments. Observing these secular democracies, leaders of religiously identified governments believe that should they incorporate democratic principles and practices into their governments, religiosity will disappear in society and leave it entirely secular, with no religious foundation. The desperation to retain their religious identity allows these regimes to justify the sacrifice of democracy.[29]

Given his sympathies both for asserting religious identity and for establishing democracies, Soroush, not surprisingly, claims that religious democracies are possible given certain conditions. First, the people must have their basic subsistence needs met. Participants in a religious democracy cannot fully utilize their reason (*'aql*) or make sense of revelation (*'shar*) if they are ill or hungry. Second, governments must willingly partake of collective wisdom. Third, governments must respect human rights.[30]

Soroush proves himself no exception to the other thinkers with regard to the necessity of material subsistence for a sustainable democracy. Maududi, Soroush, and especially Qutb find material well-being essential to democracy. Moreover, they seem to argue that economic sustainability may need to precede the establishment of democracy.[31] Without a minimum level of food, shelter, and the economic means to sustain life, people will not have the desire or the energy to devote to democracy. Soroush reasons that the first challenge in the establishment of democracy is to enable people to obtain basic goods without inordinate struggle. Only when they are not mired in poverty and insecurity do humans find the time and effort to combat injustice. Political development depends on economic development.[32]

Soroush understands that poverty impedes the development of democracy because it destroys the optimism that motivates participation in government. Poverty, accompanied by desperation and greed, and typically caused or exacerbated by corrupt governments, weakens the trust that is required of participants in a democracy. The lack of basic material goods creates an environment where people compete with each other for mere survival. Such a harsh environment, where humans cannot feel free to share and to cooperate with each other, is not conducive to democracy. Moreover, institutions essential to a functioning democracy, particularly schools, cannot feasibly be created until people are adequately nourished and sheltered. Poverty makes educating people extremely difficult. Although Soroush acknowledges that an equal distribution of wealth is not practical or perhaps even desirable, he realizes that each individual must possess a minimal level of prosperity for the establishment and sustainability of a democracy. Without even this basic level of material well-being, people cannot experience the security that allows them to take part in government without fear.[33]

Using the example of freedom of speech, Soroush demonstrates how democracy flourishes once people are capable of meeting their basic needs. Because freedom of speech allows people to protest injustices, to attend schools, and to exchange ideas, its presence and use function as an accurate barometer of a flourishing democracy. Soroush believes that economic development and a culture of idea exchange are required for people to believe that they are entitled to freedom of speech and to demand this right. When people possess the leisure time to pursue intellectual activity, freedom of speech becomes both a desire and a concern. The "time, leisure, and security" devoted to the practice of free speech, however, become possible only when people's energies are not drained in dealing with elementary needs and "where the seeds of ideas are allowed to germinate in the fertile communal soil." [34]

Open dialogue plays a significant role in the process of developing the rational systems of thought and management required of democracies.[35] Developed democracies, Soroush observes, have established popular control over the dissemination of knowledge, wealth, and power. If the entire citizenry, rather than a select few, controls the media, economy, and politics, rationality will flourish. The plurality of opinions and the consideration of others in the making of economic and political decisions contribute to the rational decisions necessary for a just, democratic government. Rational decisions, in Soroush's opinion, are just decisions. Rational decisions are not clouded by jurisprudential bias or favoritism of one faction over another. Rational decisions come about when the people consider a multitude of options and opinions and are able to draw conclusions on the basis of these choices. Democracy is the best means of establishing this process of decision making.

Other Islamic thinkers, Soroush acknowledges, assert that democracy primarily grows out of the "bourgeois mentality" and "the ethos of haggling."[36] Soroush's interlocutors associate democracy with the vulgarity of the marketplace. They conflate democracy and Western values with unfettered capitalism and greed in an attempt to discredit what they perceive as "non-Islamic" forms of government. Soroush responds to these thinkers with the claim that democracy does not develop out of the marketplace, but rather out of the desire for knowledge. For Soroush, rationality, democracy, justice, and the quest for truth are inseparable. One of these values cannot be considered without thinking of the others. Once a society meets a minimal level of material, spiritual, and intellectual well-being, establishing a democracy becomes both possible and desirable. As a society becomes more highly developed, democracy even becomes a requirement.[37] Soroush claims that, particularly for societies that display the desire for scientific advancement, democracy and the free exchange of ideas are prerequisites. A government that suppresses research and the free exchange of ideas effectively staunches the flow of scientific discovery.[38]

A democracy must remain open to the plural forms of reasoning expressed by the public. This reasoning includes both religious and nonreligious reasoning. Soroush stresses the necessity for both kinds of reasoning in a religious government. Whereas Maududi and Qutb emphasize the need to look into Islamic sources for guidance in governance, Soroush demonstrates the need for nonreligious knowledge in addition to religious reasoning. Soroush vehemently argues against religious thinkers who eschew nonreligious sources of knowledge. He admonishes these thinkers by asserting that such disregard for nonreligious reasoning is actually a breach of religious responsibility. Religion, he explains, must be subservient to the greater goal of justice; therefore, religion must support democracy because it remains the best available means to the establishment of justice. This requires that religion accommodate democracy, rather than democracy accommodate religion. The value of justice transcends religious belief. Religion must strive to become just in itself.[39]

Reliance on religious texts alone cannot sustain government, particularly in the case of Islam, where *shari'a* has diverged from faith. The written law does not equal true faith. Unlike Islamic scholars who maintain that obeying the *shari'a* proves one's Islamic faith, Soroush claims that jurisprudence is wrongly conflated with belief. He thus draws a distinction between "jurisprudential democratic government" and "religious democratic government."[40] Scholars who claim to desire Islamic democracy, in Soroush's opinion, confuse the two types of government. They write about the *law* of Islam as if it were the *religion* of Islam.[41] Many Islamic thinkers, notably Qutb, mistakenly rely on the ostensible existence and implementation of *shura* and jurisprudential tools such as *ijma*, *maslahat* (rulings in the public interest), and *ijtihad* as proof of democracy.[42]

A democratic religious government requires extrareligious reasoning, including rational findings, as a sounding board for religious belief. Rational, extrareligious knowledge functions to renew religious reasoning. The dialectical relationship between the two kinds of knowledge ensures both the continuance of religious identity and the democratic process. Democratic religious regimes need to establish religion as a guide and solution to conflict. Nevertheless, as democratic governments, such religious regimes need also to respect the reasoning of the collective with regard to religious belief.[43]

Although secular governments allow for religious diversity and religious reasoning, they do not encourage it as a form of public appeal. Government officials and participants in political debates may rely on religious reasoning in private, but they are required to use secular reasoning and secular language in public decisions. Soroush believes that a religious government, as opposed to a secular government, would not keep religious reasoning private. Religious reasoning, as well as secular and purely rational arguments, would guide public decision making. In a religious democracy, citizens and officials could use religious and secular language in the public square.

## DIVINELY DIVIDED

Several themes emerge in the discussions of Maududi, Qutb, and Soroush on democracy and equality. They address, in particular depth, the importance of material well-being, the relationship between Islam and the West, and the role of *shari'a.* Their complex stances on these topics defy the easy categorization of their ideas as "traditionalist" or "liberal." Qutb and Soroush, for instance, both stress the necessity of material goods for the establishment of popular government, despite the usual classification of Qutb as a traditionalist and Soroush as a liberal.[44] Maududi, Qutb, and Soroush agree on a profound philosophical level that Islam as practiced differs from Islam as a religion. The major topic on which these three thinkers fall along predictable lines concerns the relationship between Islam and the West. Maududi and Qutb argue vehemently against Western influence in Muslim societies, whereas Soroush views the West as one of many sources of knowledge applicable to religious governance.[45] Examining the points of divergence and convergence for these thinkers provides additional insights into the relationship between human rights and Islam.

As stated above, Qutb and Soroush agree on the priority of material well-being in the establishment of democracy (or, as Qutb might state, "popular sovereignty").[46] For these thinkers, democracy is not viable until the people are adequately fed, clothed, and sheltered. They cite various reasons for the necessity of material goods as prior to democracy. In Qutb's larger view of Islam, both the spiritual and the material well-being of a human are necessary.[47] To deprive human beings of their physical needs is not only impractical but also sacrilegious and worthy of punishment in the afterlife. Poverty devastates a person's self-esteem and renders one incapable of participating fully in a democracy. A person living in poverty cannot believe in the principle of equality, which for Qutb forms the basis of democracy.

For Soroush, material well-being also plays a foundational role in establishing democracy. Soroush emphasizes that adequate food, shelter, and clothing are necessary in order to establish the psychological and institutional bases of democracy.[48] People, in his opinion, do not desire democracy until these basic needs have been met. People who are starving, lack shelter, and are without basic human services do not possess the spirit of sharing and cooperation required for a culture of democracy. Democracy thrives in a society where people can trust one another. Economically depressed communities render its inhabitants incapable of trusting one another. Democracy is a luxury, a secondary desire that people wish to realize only after they meet their primary needs. Once the people desire democracy, their material well-being remains important because it is necessary for continued participation in democratic institutions, such as schools and a free press. Soroush goes even further than Qutb in stating that once people are taken care of materially and have the desire to participate in government, then democracy becomes vital to their survival. The free exchange of ideas takes place most effectively in a democracy.

None of these thinkers considers the alternative view that democracy enables governments to take care of the material goods of the people. Although the views of Qutb and Soroush seem reasonable, the prioritizing of economic necessity over democracy oversimplifies the relationship between wealth and civil rights. Moreover, such views are often exploited by dictatorial regimes. Authoritarian leaders such as Lee Kuan Yew of Singapore have defended government curtailment of civil rights in order to expedite economic reforms. Economist Amartya Sen, however, has demonstrated that democracy may actually improve the material conditions of citizens. Democratic institutions, especially a free press, help to prevent gross catastrophes such as famine by keeping checks on government negligence.[49] People's material needs may be met through the establishment of democracy first, rather than the other way around.

That both Qutb and Soroush consider the material forces a priority for historical change requires a reconsideration of the division between conservative traditionalist and liberal intellectual. According to this common categorization, one hallmark that divides the two camps concerns the sources of their ideologies.[50] Intellectual liberals are open to the ideas that come out of Western and Christian sources, whereas the conservative traditionalists claim that their ideas derive exclusively from Islamic texts and traditions. Both Qutb and Soroush, for example, appear to incorporate Marx's major ideas on materialism into their thinking.[51] Although this is perhaps not surprising in an analysis of Soroush's works, it seems initially counterintuitive when one discusses the ideas of Qutb. Soroush, who advocates the incorporation of ideas from any source regardless of its religious, political, or ethnic origin, often cites the ideas of European thinkers.[52] That he draws from Marx is typical of his intellectual style. Qutb, however, who expresses strong anti-Western views, indeed even to the extent of avoiding the Western term "democracy," aims to convince his audience that his ideas derive solely from the Qur'an, *sunna,* and *hadith.*[53]

Although the Qur'an addresses the need of human beings for material well-being, it does not provide enough information such that Qutb could extrapolate as much as he does on the topic of materialism and poverty in his writings. The significance of attributing one's ideas to Western writers, however, lies not in whether one actually uses their thoughts but in the reluctance or willingness to credit them. Qutb believes that by attributing his ideas to Islam, he will instill pride and confidence into a community that has been demoralized and forced into submission by Western colonizers. Soroush, although critical of secular governments typically associated with the West, is concerned primarily with problems of plurality, not only among people of different traditions but also among people who are religious and who are not.

Another area that Qutb and Soroush both address, indeed an area that all three thinkers consider, concerns the relationship between Islam as practiced and Islam as a religion. All thinkers observe a discrepancy between what Muslims understand as Islam and the way in which they should understand Islam. Maududi, Qutb, and Soroush understand Islam as a belief system that encompasses the whole of life. Material well-being, governance, law, rituals, knowledge, and truth—these are components of Islam that should not be separated from one another. These thinkers express the greatest criticism when Muslims confuse one component of Islam for the whole of Islam.

Qutb stresses that his campaign against poverty, for example, is not economic or political, but religious. Islam, unlike other religions, especially Christianity, and unlike communism, seeks the unity of the material with the spiritual. Whereas Christianity stresses the spiritual and communism the material, Islam acknowledges that humans are creatures of both spirit and flesh and does not ask its followers to deny either part of their being. Although others may see the fight for equitable wealth distribution as a form of secular governance, Qutb views this act as a religious one, demanded by Islam and demonstrated through the practice of *zakat*.[54]

Qutb also understands popular government through the lens of Islam. The notion of *shura* arises out of divine precedent, rather than political philosophy, even if similar ideas may be found there.[55] Likewise, just rule and obedience to government are not purely political principles, but religious ones. The attempt to separate the political processes from an Islamic way of life would be, for Qutb, un-Islamic.

Maududi and Qutb agree in their chastisement of Muslims for separating political life from religious life. Maududi laments the rise of government leaders who view their positions in terms of political expediency rather than religious duty. The command to rule justly, to command good and forbid evil, comes out of the Qur'an and the practices of the Prophet. Government leaders often fail to meet even this most basic level of morality, much less live up to Islamic ideals. Maududi blames Muslim citizens for failing to hold their leaders up to their religious duties.[56] He explains that citizens who go through the motions of religious practice, such as going to mosque, praying, giving *zakat,* and making the *hajj,* do not understand that those actions alone are insufficient to make a person a good Muslim. Religious rituals in and of themselves, without a greater awareness and participation in the community, constitute only one part of Islam. The failure of political leaders and citizens to see the unity of Islam underlies much of Maududi's writings on Islamic democracy.

Soroush also seeks the alignment of religion with politics, though the religion need not necessarily be Islam. In the case of Islamic governments, religion and politics have not been melded properly. The proponents of *shari'a* confuse jurisprudential governance for religious governance. He explicitly denounces the role of *shari'a* and tools of Islamic governance, such as *shura*, whereas both Maududi and Qutb defend *shari'a* and traditional jurisprudential concepts. Likewise, Soroush refutes claims that the use of *shura*, as well as legal tools such as *ijma*, constitutes democracy.[57] A truly democratic government is one in which the people share control over all facets of society, including the media, wealth, and political leadership. Soroush does not believe that the traditional tools of Islamic governance have historically guaranteed these aspects of a democratic society.

Soroush takes a different approach than either Maududi or Qutb to "secular" political theories. Rather than reject them as similar, but ultimately false imitations of Islam, as Qutb does, Soroush views these theories as necessary to figuring out a greater universal truth.[58] Religion benefits from the debate with secular theories. In fact, he considers secular, rational views as necessary within a religious democracy. Without them, there would be no check on religious views gone astray. Because secular views and religious views all aim to seek the same goal, that is, some ultimate truth, they should work together in this endeavor.

Soroush, unlike Maududi or Qutb, displays a strong faith in rationality. He views religion as distinct from our rational capacity to understand religion but understands that religion and reason converse with each other in attempts to uncover the truth. Reason does not complement religion but rather "struggles to improve its own understanding of religion."[59] Religion, as divine, remains constant; however, human reason and interpretations of the religious change over time. Soroush often analogizes the distinction and the relationship between religion and religious knowledge as similar to the natural world and science.[60] The truths of the natural world (such as the laws of physics), like religion, do not change; however, human understanding of the natural world changes through history. Our comprehension of the laws of gravity, for example, differs from the way humans understood the laws of gravity a millennia ago. Gravity has not changed since then, but our knowledge of it is different. In distinguishing between human reason and religion, Soroush diverges with Maududi and Qutb, who understand human reason as untrustworthy compared to divine revelation. Soroush's theory of interpretation enables him to draw differences between genuine *shari'a* and the unjust application of *shari'a* in Islamic governments, whereas for Maududi and Qutb any critique of *shari'a* must be generated from within the Islamic tradition itself.

These thinkers express dissatisfaction with the disjunction of Islam from other aspects of life. They all note in particular the separation of Islam as a religion from politics and the separation of religious ritual from an Islamic worldview. The three thinkers, however, diverge with regard to the means by which Islam and politics should be reunited. Maududi, Qutb, and Soroush all see the Qur'an as a historical text, although the ways in which they interpret the historicity of the text differ. Maududi and Qutb see the text as a hearkening to a time past, whereas Soroush views the text as containing historical information in addition to principles that humans apply through time.

Maududi and Qutb desire a return, even an escape, to the days of the beginnings of Islam, when the Prophet ruled both religiously and politically. They also seek wisdom in the *shari'a* and the early jurisprudential writings of Muslim scholars. As a result, when they write in contemporary times of the separation of religion from politics, they aim to return as much as possible to a golden age of Islam, when people lived by the words of the Prophet and *shari'a.* They look to the Qur'an, the *sunna,* and the *hadith,* as well as to the writings on law and legal method that were recorded prior to the tenth century. They hope to reunite religion and politics using the past as their guide.[61]

Soroush, on the other hand, also seeks the reunion of religion and politics, but does not seek a return to the days of the past in the same way that Maududi and Qutb do.[62] Although he uses the Qur'an as a guide, he also incorporates modern views on religion and politics, including secular and rational thought. Instead of returning to the past, he believes that religion and politics can be unified in a contemporary way that differs from the way in which Islam existed in its formative period. He accepts the realities of the present day and attempts to accommodate facts such as cultural pluralism, technology, and globalism into a union of religion and politics. The Qur'an is only one of many texts that contain certain timeless principles applicable to the present age.

Although the three thinkers appear to agree to a certain extent on larger themes of economic justice and the union of religion and politics, they disagree to a great extent on the relationship between Islam and the West. Maududi and Qutb express strong anti-Western sentiments, whereas Soroush is open to ideas from the West. Both in methodology and in content, the three thinkers reveal how they approach the West and its ideas.

Maududi and Qutb view the West as immoral in its very foundations and in the way in which it treats people. The West, particularly in the forms of Christianity, capitalism, and communism, violates the fundamental belief of Islam that the body and spirit are unified. The divide of the body from the spirit, and the political from the religious, leads to the immorality that Maududi and Qutb see in the West. Qutb writes about the immoral ways in which the West treats women in the name of emancipation and points to the discrimination and slaughter by the American government of Native Americans and Africans.[63] Maududi expresses his anti-Westernism also through comparison. He favors Islamic democracy over Western democracy because Islamic democracies are divinely guided, whereas Western democracies are determined by the selfish desires of the individuals who constitute them.[64] Maududi and Qutb see the influence of the West into Islamic culture as a stain to what was once pristine.

While both Maududi and Qutb express anti-Western sentiment in their writings, they also attempt to bolster the image of Islam. In the form of apologetics, they write about the ways in which Islam, when its true vision is seen, creates a perfectly just world, free of poverty, immorality, and suffering. They glorify the past of Islam, stressing only the positive aspects of its history and explaining the benefits of a return to the rule of *shari'a.* In tandem with their disparaging of the West, these writings aim to instill pride into Muslims who have been dominated by Western imperialists and forced into adopting aspects of Western culture.

Soroush does not disparage Western culture, and while remaining critical of secular governance, adopts Western ideas and incorporates these into his own writings. In an essay on religious exclusivity, for example, Soroush considers the ideas of Karl Barth, John Hick, Carl Jung, Ninian Smart, Emile Brunner, and Arnold Toynbee, in addition to quoting from Hafez and Rumi.[65] He believes that morality and justice can be expressed in a variety of ways, through different religions and cultures and through time. More important, he asserts that he can do so without compromising an Islamic faith. He understands the truth of Islam to be ultimately coincidental to the truths expressed in Christianity and in Western law and philosophy.

That Soroush believes he can harmonize religious beliefs with other beliefs may result from any number of reasons. The typical explanations, such as exposure to Western education and culture or the lack of subjection to colonial threat, do not suffice, however. Although Soroush studied Western thought, the same can be said of Maududi and Qutb. In fact, Qutb's time in the United States helped to convince him of the immorality of the West, especially with regard to the behavior and treatment of women. Maududi and Qutb both hail from countries with legacies of colonialism, which may explain their deep aversion to the West, but Soroush witnessed the influence of American CIA involvement in

Iran. These factors, perhaps partially responsible for the directions of their thought, are not sufficient to explain the vast differences among the thinkers.

Though this inquiry may turn into a hopelessly circular debate, the question of why some Muslim thinkers develop anti-Western sentiment and some do not may be answered partially by examining the ideas within Islam that these thinkers choose to emphasize. Given the immensity of the tradition, its depth in history and its breadth across cultures, many different subtraditions exist within Islam, any one or combination of which may have influenced the ideas of these thinkers.[66] Soroush's emphasis on rationalism, for instance, may stem partially from the thought of the early Mu'tazilites, who incorporated Greek philosophy into their ethics of Islam in the eighth through tenth centuries.[67] The opponents of the rationalists, the Ash'arites, who believe that we can only know definitively the rightness or wrongness of actions through divine revelation, may appeal to Maududi and Qutb.[68] These ethical foundations, rather than the Qur'an itself, lead to interpretations that express relative degrees of openness to non-Islamic traditions. The Mu'tazilites, who considered themselves Islamic theologians, adopted Hellenic philosophical frameworks but filled the content with Muslim ideals. Hence, a Mu'tazilite thinker might have adopted a teleological structure to define human life, but substituted union with God, instead of *eudaimonia,* as an end. Not surprisingly, voluntarists, including Ash'arites, found the works of Mu'tazilites blasphemous because of the heavy emphasis on human rationality as opposed to divine revelation. They argued that human rationality was insufficient to understand the will of God. The only way to determine God's will was through strict interpretation of the Qur'an, *sunna,* and *hadith.* This view resonates with the determination of Maududi and Qutb to rely solely on divine scripture for their ideas and to return to divinely inspired law in the form of *shari'a,* as opposed to secular law based on human reason.

The ideas of the Mu'tazilites and the Ash'arites, although they existed long before the births of Maududi, Qutb, and Soroush, seem to echo through these thinkers' writings. Particularly with regard to the stated use of non-Islamic texts and to the openness of human reason, these contemporary thinkers display the variety of Islamic influences in their writings. In their discussions on freedom of conscience and toleration, as in their works on democracy, they continue to demonstrate this complexity of Islamic thought.

# —4—

# The Free Conscience

## *"No Compulsion in Religion"*

By engaging in dialogue with Maududi, Qutb, and Soroush on the subject matter of freedom of conscience, we begin to see this human right from new perspectives based in Islamic thought. We commence with the fortunate agreement that freedom of conscience is, indeed, a human right, but how one comes to this conclusion varies. The particulars of freedom of conscience differ according to each thinker and the unique context in which he understands this human right. That we understand the paths these Islamic thinkers take to their conclusions about freedom of conscience and the nuanced ways in which they comprehend this right is essential to the possibility of coming to an agreement—a fusion of horizons—about human rights.

As with the concepts of democracy and, as we will see, toleration, Maududi, Qutb, and Soroush claim that freedom of conscience is a human right found within Islam. In their more apologetic moments, Maududi and Qutb claim that Islam is superior to other religious and political systems in its early observance and command to respect the free conscience of other human beings. The three thinkers, however, differ in the ways in which they assess and analyze freedom of conscience within the Islamic tradition. Soroush situates freedom in general, and freedom of conscience in particular, within his larger understanding of the unity of truth that can be found in multiple religions. Freedom of conscience is necessary to deepen not only our knowledge of Islam but also our knowledge of the world in general. Maududi and Qutb proclaim the uniqueness, rather than the universality, of Islam and defend their religious tradition as a protector of conscience against the evils of the West. Soroush shares with Maududi and Qutb the criticism that the West abuses freedom. Although Qutb prefers to protect Muslims from Western abuse of freedom by restricting their exposure to the West, Soroush believes that the misunderstandings of the West can be clarified only through a freer exchange of ideas.

Freedom of conscience emerges as a motif across major religious traditions, including Islam.[1] Like democracy and toleration, freedom of conscience exists as a fundamental human right and is upheld as an ideal—at least theoretically—across cultures. In a democracy, freedom of conscience is the foundation on which popular participation in government is based. Citizens are expected to, and trust that they safely can, express their conscience as it relates to their government in elections, media, and other public forums. Freedom of conscience shares with religious toleration the idea that the uniqueness of each human being should be respected. The two rights complement each other in that toleration describes outward behaviors toward internal beliefs.[2]

Muslims often vaunt the Qur'anic injunction: "There is no compulsion in religion" (2:256). The profound recognition that faith cannot be imposed on others is the basis of Islamic claims of religious toleration. If one cannot compel another toward belief in a different faith, then one must accept religious difference. One must also recognize that divine, and not human, factors determine faith. The acceptance of "no compulsion" sets Islam apart from other religions that attempt to evangelize others instead of tolerating people's beliefs in different faith traditions. Historically, of course, Muslims have not always lived up to the ideal of religious toleration. Nonetheless, the oft-quoted Qur'anic verse has served as a reminder that God does not sanction religious compulsion.

Any community that attempts to govern its members, whether as participants of a faith tradition or as citizens of a state, must wrestle with the inherent problems of freedom of conscience and its expression. Although people ideally maintain their memberships in such communities out of free will, the free conscience and its attendant forms of expression also serve as sources of criticism, falsehoods, and even the destruction of those very communities. Communities must determine the extent to which the expression of free conscience may exist unfettered without causing critical damage to other members of the community or to the community itself. Communities must balance the negative aspects of the freedoms of expression and conscience with the knowledge that voices of criticism bring to light the ills of a community and help to correct its wrongs. Freedom of conscience, although it may continue to exist even within totalitarian regimes, flourishes in a free and creative society. The healthy development of ideas exists in cultures where open exchanges of thoughts and beliefs are allowed to nourish one another.

## CONSCIENCE IN CULTURAL CONTEXT

Maududi's writings on freedom of conscience appear at first glance extraordinarily tolerant, given his known anti-Western and pro-Islamic polemics. In part because he writes from the Indian subcontinent, where Muslims comprise a minority among a majority of Hindus, he writes in a context that differs from that of Qutb's majority-Muslim Egypt or Soroush's majority-Muslim Iran. Maududi, because he speaks as a minority voice, must consider carefully how Muslims in Pakistan and India should negotiate their status as one of several religious groups living within a shared geographic region. Maududi cannot write about freedom of conscience using a simple Islam versus West model; rather, he writes with an eye toward accommodating the variety of religious beliefs and practices found on the subcontinent.

Maududi addresses the major aspects of freedom of conscience, including the right to freedom of religious belief, practice, organization, and expression. He states forcefully, "Islam has given the right to the individual that his religious sentiments will be given due respect and nothing will be said or done which may encroach upon this right." Beginning with Islamic law, which addresses freedom of conscience from the perspective of a Muslim ruler, Maududi refers to Qur'anic injunctions against compulsion in religion and laws regarding *dhimmis,* the People of the Book who traditionally were entitled to protection under law. He claims simultaneously that Islam is the greatest of religions, that Muslims should encourage people to accept Islam, and that Muslims should not use force or otherwise compel non-Muslims to embrace Islam. People should accept Islam through their own free choice, not through compulsion. Even though Maududi believes in the superiority of Islam, he insists that if persons elect not to embrace Islam, Muslims must avoid placing political or social pressure on them to convert. Rather, Muslims are obligated to acknowledge and respect their decision. With regard to Jews and Christians, Maududi advises Muslims by quoting the Qur'an: "Do not argue with the people of the Book unless it is in the politest manner" (29:46). He explains that Islam does not recommend even using hurtful words and language against people who hold convictions with which Muslims disagree.[3]

Non-Muslims, for example, may openly discuss and criticize Islam. Muslims should respect the freedom of non-Muslims to criticize Islam to the extent allowed within civil law. So long as non-Muslims in their remarks about Islam abide by laws that are applicable to all citizens, those remarks must be tolerated.[4] Maududi anticipates that Muslims will take offense at the discussion and criticism of Islam by non-Muslims but insists on respecting the freedom of conscience and its application. Limitations on the use of force, either verbal or physical, concerning matters of faith are very stringent.

The safeguarding of privacy shares similarities with the protection of freedom of conscience. In both cases, a boundary exists separating the spheres of the state and the private life of the individual. The state must pass a very high threshold in order to interfere legitimately with the private life of the citizen. In his discussions on freedom, Maududi notes Qur'anic verses and *hadith* that ensure the limitations of the state on the individual: "'Do not spy on one another' (49:12). 'Do not enter any houses except your own homes unless you are sure of their occupants' consent' (24:27).'"[5] On the basis of these sources, Maududi argues for limitations on the state to interfere in the private life of its citizens.

A government may only take away a person's freedom for reasons that the public knowingly and fully endorses. In one *hadith* that Maududi cites, Muhammad releases an imprisoned man because the charges for his arrest were not made public. Maududi goes so far as to state that governments cannot justify espionage simply by stating that such intrusion on the privacy of individuals is necessary.[6] Governments must present an extraordinarily persuasive case to the public in order to justify spying into the private life of a citizen; neither a blanket statement concerning security nor a person's dangerous profile offers sufficient warrant to infringe on a person's privacy.

The idea of freedom of conscience accommodates anyone who is a citizen, which includes Hindus as well as Jews and Christians. Maududi applies to all humans the command to respect freedom of conscience, summarized in the frequently quoted Qur'anic phrase, "There shall be no coercion in the matter of faith" (2:256). "This order," he asserts, "is not merely limited to the People of the Scriptures, but applies with equal force to those following other faiths."[7] He cites the Qur'an: "Do not abuse those they appeal to instead of God" (6:108). This is particularly important when one discusses Hindus, as Jews and Christians have traditionally been understood by Muslims to worship the same Abrahamic God.[8] Establishing that all persons are entitled to freedom of conscience with regard specifically to religious belief, Maududi relates this to free religious practice and expression. *Dhimmis* are entitled to freedom of conscience and therefore have the freedom also to exercise that freedom in the form of religious ritual and ceremony. This right to freedom of conscience and belief is irrevocable. Unless the *dhimmis* denounce their citizenship, they are entitled to these rights.[9] Traditional Islamic rules concerning *dhimmis*, as well as contemporary notions of citizenship, both favor the protection of religious practice.

Although most of Maududi's writings on freedom of conscience do not directly place limits on belief, expression, or practice for non-Muslims, he insists on a different standard for Muslims and the Islamic state on the basis of the Qur'anic injunction to enjoin the good and forbid evil (9:71).[10] If any state does not allow Muslims to carry out this injunction, then it is restricting Muslims' right to believe and practice freely.[11] A government that disallows freedom of belief and practice would stand in conflict with divine mandates that permit religious freedom.[12] Maududi asserts that freedom of conscience is a conditional right that must be asserted responsibly. Beyond the generally uncontroversial claim that states should limit violent expressions of faith or conscience, Maududi argues that Islamic states in particular should expect that freedom of expression be limited for the dissemination of good.[13] Islam grants freedom of conscience on the grounds that its citizens claim this right responsibly. It should uphold "virtue and truth" and disavow "evil and wickedness."[14] The propagation of good and condemnation of evil are, in fact, obligatory in Islam.

Only God can know a person's conscience; however, outward expressions of the conscience can be known and regulated by other humans. Freedom of association, which is often an essential component of freedom of religious belief, should therefore be exercised with the aim of promoting goodness and righteousness and denouncing "evil and mischief." Maududi does not define evil or mischief, but one can easily imagine the abuse of those definitions by an intolerant government. A group that meets to discuss the absence of God, for instance, or debates the lack of proof for monotheism could be branded as spreading "evil." Maududi elaborates that although Islam does not restrict religious debate and dialogue, it does demand that these conversations meet a certain level of "decency."[15] Again, Maududi does not elaborate on the definition of "decency," but as with the terms "evil" and "mischief," the misuse of such a term by the state could severely restrict citizens' freedom.

Along similar lines, Maududi makes the ambiguous claim that Muslims have an obligation to prevent people from doing evil.[16] The abuse of this obligation, also undefined, could conceivably lead to Muslims preventing people from practicing religious beliefs that appear subjectively "evil." The injunction to propagate the good and forbid evil ostensibly appears a benign divine order, but in the context of freedom of conscience, it could curb freedoms relevant to the free practice of religious belief. Maintaining a balance between freedom of conscience and the injunction to promote the good and forbid evil presents challenges that Maududi fails to overcome.

Despite the latent dangers in his particular interpretation of Islam concerning freedom of conscience, Maududi insists that the Islamic concept of freedom of conscience is superior to that found in the West.[17] Europe and the United States, Maududi argues, have become too relaxed in their upholding of moral virtue. Although the West upholds freedom of conscience, belief, practice, association, and expression, it does so in an irresponsible way such that these freedoms actually corrupt society. Maududi believes that the abuse of these freedoms by Western peoples and the states that govern them lead to the ironic effect of curbing freedom. Muslims, specifically, can no longer exist as devout Muslims in such an evil environment. The sex- and violence-filled media and the lifestyle of women found in the West prevent Muslims from living the kind of life Islam prescribes. Freedom of conscience and its associated freedoms impinge on the ability of Muslims to practice their religion freely.

There is a trade-off between freedom of conscience and the command to propagate the good and forbid evil. The West has gone too far in the former direction, Maududi believes, and an Islamic state might be able to reverse this trend. The Western threshold for freedom of expression, which generally limits expression only if it directly leads to violence or is in itself violent, is incapable of protecting virtue. The consequentialist view that freedoms of conscience and expression will eventually lead to the rise of good ideas and the demise of bad ones—a view that Soroush espouses—plays no role in Maududi's thought. He takes a much darker view of the repercussions of human freedom without restraint. Darwinian theory applied to the realm of ideas assumes a much too optimistic position on human influences. Speaking from a point of view that sees the West as the most powerful, yet unjust, cultural influence in the world, Maududi gives little credit to the position that the good will prevail in the end.

## THE PARADOX OF FREEDOM

Freedom of conscience, for Qutb, is essential to the social justice that defines Islam. He refers to freedom of conscience as "the principle cornerstone . . . for the building of social justice . . . on which all the others must rest."[18] As the conscience becomes increasingly free, there is greater evidence of social and economic equality; with greater social and economic justice, people's consciences move toward greater freedom. As with many dialectical models, however, Qutb's understanding of the relationship between the free conscience and justice often appears contradictory. Moreover, given Qutb's epistemology, the free conscience also seems ironically limited. When people's consciences choose to be guided by some force other than an Islamic concept of God, they become, according to Qutb, unable to discern the elements of social justice.

Not all people are capable of handling the great responsibility required of freedom of belief and expression, Qutb believes. Those whose minds and hearts have been tainted by corrupt cultures, as those found in the West, are not truly free. These people suffer something akin to the Marxist notion of false consciousness, or the condition under which people support a powerful and misguided ideology to their own detriment.[19] The free conscience should be grounded in an interpretation of the Qur'an and *shari'a* that defines freedom of conscience relative to God.

In his analysis of freedom of conscience and social justice, Qutb explains that only "inner conviction of spirit" can assure a complete and permanent social justice. Islam educates the conscience by integrating material needs as well as spiritual desires, rather than separating them or privileging one aspect of human life over the other. In contrast to Christianity, capitalism, and communism, Islam satisfies the free conscience because it addresses the needs of both the soul and the body. Qutb implies that a religion or ideology that privileges one part of the human above the other constricts the conscience. The conscience, when guided by Christianity, is not free because it is bound to the spirit at the expense of the body. Capitalism and communism guide the conscience into considering only the material life, that is, only the body, not the spirit. The free conscience, which Islam alone can nurture, embraces the unity of the spiritual and the material. This union is especially important because it provides the freedom to pursue issues of social justice. If one aspect of humanity, for example, the material, is considered the more important, then issues of spiritual justice are demoted. Likewise, if the spiritual is considered to be more important than the material, then issues of material justice are demoted. The integrated understanding of conscience, which is sensitive to both spiritual and bodily goods, is both freeing and practical in its flexibility to respond to injustice in all its forms. The concept of unity refers not simply to the spirit and to the body, but also to the community. Islam stresses the importance of joining together as a community for establishing economic justice in particular. Freedom of conscience speaks to the need for "the unity and mutual responsibility of the community."[20]

This concern with the unity of spirit and body for the conscience reflects a compelling concern with social and economic equality. Qutb asserts that the notion of equality has its roots in freedom of conscience. Although persons clearly possess greater or lesser physical and intellectual talents, God grants to all alike the instinct of freedom of conscience. Everyone, regardless of rank or wealth, stands equal before God. Nonetheless, equality of freedom of conscience does not substitute for equality of social and economic status. Qutb asserts that if this instinct for freedom of conscience is cultivated among both the powerful and the disempowered, then the result will be a massive move toward equilibrium, marked by an empowering of the weak and a disempowering of the powerful.[21]

Islam demands that the human conscience submit only to God and not to other human beings. This submission to God forms the basis of a radical equality that prevents Muslims from worshipping even the prophets as anything greater than human. Qutb notes that Muhammad himself is merely a messenger and that when he, like the prophets before him, passed away, no one was to give up his faith in God.[22] The association of anything or anyone, including prophets, as God prevents the conscience from associating freely and fully with the divine. When the conscience is oppressed and not free to submit to the divine, it creates categories of inequality wherein some things and persons are considered greater than others.

This theological approach to freedom of conscience, although highly egalitarian, also places limits that appear ironically to restrict one's intellectual and spiritual freedom. Wary of Muslims' adulation of the West and Western culture, Qutb believes that Muslims should not learn about their approaches to the humanities and social sciences.[23] He fears that the association of Westerners and Western culture with the divine inhibits Muslims' proper worship of God alone. Learning about Western thought perpetuates the cultural imperialism of the Europeans. Instead, Muslims should study their own religious texts and the writings of their own peoples. The hard sciences, however, are grudgingly exempt from the cultural biases of the West and should be studied by Muslims in order to help their countries to advance technologically. Qutb neither espouses cultural exchange as a means of social progress nor believes that technology and culture progress in tandem.

Freedom of expression, or the outward proof of freedom of conscience, is scrutinized according to Qutb's epistemological distinctions. For Qutb, Muslims who express European cultural ideas or support

Western ideas of progress and equality are victims of colonialism and unwitting collaborators in their own cultural demise. Freedom of conscience, according to Qutb, develops best in an environment shielded from foreign influence.

The radical equality that Qutb describes as originating from the concept of freedom of conscience requires Muslims to restrict their exposure to foreign religions and cultures. Qutb deeply distrusts Europe and the United States, but he also does not trust Muslims to be capable of judging for themselves between the beneficial and the harmful. The legacy of colonialism in Egypt and North Africa, the Levant, the Arabian Peninsula, and the Indian subcontinent affirms his fears of Western, Christian hostility toward Muslims. Any suggestion that cultural exchange with the Christian West might lead to progress and justice would be met with decades of historical evidence to the contrary. Qutb's extremely protectionist stance toward Islam and Islamic culture arises directly as a response to this history. His protectiveness, however, seems at times patriarchal to such an extent that it belies his message of equality of freedom of conscience. Qutb avoids the question of Muslims being capable of judging or determining for themselves their own ideal route to progress, justice, and freedom. He alone seems to have escaped the false consciousness that the colonialists use to perpetuate their cultural rule.

Although Qutb argues that the theological grounds of equality and social and economic justice work together toward a common good, his version of freedom of conscience also makes possible a kind of quietism that suggests otherwise. He explains that with the free conscience, one should not worry about the acquisition of food, shelter, or clothing, for God will provide for those things. One should feel no fear for one's position in life, or death, or injury, or poverty. Indeed, once Muslims fully realize freedom of conscience, they will find themselves independent of the material things in life and will escape from the oppressive nature of money and social status.[24] Qutb argues that if one is fully accepting of the supremacy of God alone, then such fears become unsubstantiated.

The demand for social change and the motivation for technological progress do not appear necessary according to this characterization of the free conscience. Yet, Qutb also argues that the presence of social inequity and poverty is evidence of the lack of faith. Although a good Muslim would not allow such things to happen, when such injustices do occur, the free conscience should fight for and defend social justice and equality.[25] Qutb walks a fine line between accepting one's state as God given and asserting one's right to a fair and just existence as a creature of God. The free conscience is required to acknowledge the demands of justice, and yet justice is required for the conscience to be truly free.

## THE END OF RELIGIOUS HYPOCRISY

Soroush's understanding of religious society and freedom of conscience relates directly to his attempts to clarify the role of Islam in a clerical state such as Iran. Islam, he argues, differs from *shari'a.*[26] Islamic law has been exploited by Muslim clerics, government officials, and jurists to mean religion when, in fact, law is not the same thing as religion. One fundamental difference between religion and law is that genuine acceptance of religion requires freedom of conscience, but submission to the laws of a state does not make any such demand on the conscience, only on the behavior of citizens. Therefore, the guarantee of freedom of conscience is necessary for a religious democratic society, but not for a jurisprudential society. Although a jurisprudential religious government could, albeit disingenuously, require the practice of a particular religion or punish apostasy, a religious democratic government would not condone such imposition of belief.[27] A religious society consists of true believers, whereas a society grounded in jurisprudence under the guise of religion controls its citizens without consideration of their actual beliefs.

Especially critical of Islamic jurisprudential regimes that claim to be religious societies, Soroush asserts that a religious society of any kind must first and foremost safeguard freedom of religion. A genuinely religious society consists of individuals who voluntarily identify themselves as believers of religion. Such a society distinguishes itself from a merely tyrannical regime whose citizens only claim religious belief out of fear of state punishment. Society governed by religious law may require its citizens to behave in a particular way and to express their "religiosity" in prescribed manners, but it cannot truthfully claim that its citizens are sincere believers.

Islamic governments that claim to rule by religious law are not religious societies, but tyrannies. "To compel individuals to confess a faith falsely; to paralyze minds by indoctrination, propaganda, and intimidation; and to shut down the gates of criticism, revision, and modification so that everyone would succumb to a single ideology creates not a religious society, but a monolithic and terrified mass of crippled, submissive, and hypocritical subjects." Soroush observes that people may act as if they believe in a religion. They may dress as religious authorities prescribe, perform religious rituals, and attend services so as to conform to law. Nevertheless, people inevitably believe in different things in different ways. These internally held beliefs and ideas are beyond the control of the state. Soroush analogizes different varieties of faith to wildflowers: "Like wild flowers in nature, faith will grow and flourish wherever it wishes and in whatever fragrance and color it pleases."[28]

Drawing on his understanding of the godly origin of faith, Soroush claims that religious law can only be just when it considers the divine nature of freedom of conscience. Religious law should not be based on a hubristic misunderstanding of the dynamics of religious belief. Because God is the source of faith and the cause of whether and what people choose to believe, religious law that assumes human control in matters of faith is misguided. Religious law that claims, even implicitly, that humans can determine the extent and form of others' beliefs denies the role of God in the creation of human belief. When religious leaders, clerics, and jurists create and enforce laws that they argue reveal the religiosity or apostasy of citizens, they intrude on a domain that belongs to God. Soroush asks, "What authenticity and ground would religious law have if it disregarded the freedom of faith and the humanity of understanding, refused to base its precepts upon these, and neglected to harmonize its regulations with them?"[29] Soroush points out the hypocrisy of religious laws that claim to be divinely inspired, when in actuality they oppose the flourishing of authentic religious belief.

Ironically, freedom of conscience allows people ultimately to submit to religious authority. Islamic governments desire that their citizens obey their particular version of religious belief; however, their sentiments and strategy work against their stated goals. Although Soroush agrees that a religious people would constitute a great nation, he also believes that people need to discover their religious faith through free will, not government coercion. Indeed, the best societies are those in which people are freely religious. The greatest blessing for humankind is religious belief obtained through the free will.[30]

Human beings, when they create rules for a society, can attempt to guarantee only freedom, the necessary precondition for faith. In the absence of divine grace, humans in their power can offer freedom so as to enable the receiving of grace. Governments express this highest form of humanity by making possible the acceptance of God's gift of grace. Totalitarian regimes that inhibit freedom can never claim to be divine or to reach the heights of humanity.[31] Given that humans cannot create religious societies directly, they must strive to create free ones, which enable the development of religious citizens.

Religious knowledge generated by conversation, research, and practice develops, much like scientific knowledge, where there is freedom to explore and experiment. Clerics of Islamic regimes that curtail religious freedom, but encourage scientific experimentation, create a false dichotomy between religious knowledge and scientific knowledge. On one hand, these leaders desire scientific and technological progress and therefore allow scientists to conduct research with relatively fewer restrictions than found in more humanistic fields.[33] On the other hand, they fear the research and conversation about alternative worldviews generated through the free exercise of conscience, and so they limit freedom of religion and speech.

The distinction between humanistic and scientific knowledge, which Qutb vehemently supports, Soroush finds preposterous. If there is a perceived conflict between different worldviews described in the scientific or cultural literature of non-Islamic societies, then there should be greater, not less, freedom to investigate such differences. Confusion and doubt require that more dialogues take place, not fewer.[34] When the ideas of the West appear wrong, then the freedom to investigate these flaws should be available to the people to understand and correct. To cloak ideas with a simple claim of their falsehood does nothing to illuminate the truth.

Islamic regimes that in practice limit religious freedom out of fear of apostasy in fact limit the discovery of truth. What the leaders of Islamic regimes fail to realize is that freedom, with all the deception and corruption it may bring, is also necessary for the flowering of faith and knowledge. Soroush insists that God intends for humans to be free. Those who believe that freedom blinds people to the truth fail to realize that freedom is the greatest truth.[35]

The problems found in free societies are not lost on Soroush. Although free societies enable religious belief, they also produce lies, slander, and indecency. Freedom in this way is much like reason: both have flaws and imperfections, but both also reward their seekers with greater knowledge. Reason and freedom may produce undesired results, but should never be confused with them. Reason and freedom are distinguishable from their products. The defense of freedom "is like defending a sun that shines on everything—even the waste—or a holy fire that may consume even the sacred pages of the *Mathnavi*."[36]

One must trust in freedom's ability to bring about truth and faith. Trust in freedom is evidence of faith in God. Rulers who curb freedom out of fear display a lack of trust in God. Liars and abusers of freedom should not overcome those who have faith in the ultimate goodness of freedom. Soroush states, "We must perform our duties, struggle and wage *jihad* against falsehoods, and put our trust in God." Critics who attempt to restrict freedom and the growth of ideas do not understand their own reliance on freedom. Soroush defends the truth of the saying 'One must tolerate the enemies, except the enemies of tolerance' by arguing, "An ignorant critic of this wise maxim has said that this constitutes an unwarranted exception to the maxim of freedom. Indeed, this is not an exception, but the main rule of the game."[37]

In arguing for freedom, Soroush not only acknowledges its ill use but also its dual nature. Freedom consists of both internal freedom and external freedom. These correspond roughly to freedom of conscience and freedom of action. Both are necessary for a religious democracy. Some societies focus on the latter and pay little attention to the former. Although external freedom is certainly important, it cannot be fully realized until people achieve internal freedom. People may act and behave freely, but those motions are not fully imbued with meaning until people comprehend the ways in which external freedom may represent internal freedom, particularly in the form of religious belief.

When inner freedom serves as the foundation for faith, and that faith informs one's actions, then both types of freedom, internal and external, flourish. The West places too great an emphasis on external freedom, while placing little stress on the importance of internal freedom. If internal freedoms are not encouraged, then external freedoms will not be appreciated. Colonialism and other physical manifestations of nationalist arrogance reveal how little the Western world understands the dynamic between external and internal freedoms. Unfortunately, the influence of Western society has convinced non-Westerners that external freedom is the more important of the two. Rather than simply denounce the external freedom portrayed by the West, however, non-Westerners should supplement external freedom with internal freedoms rooted in their own cultures. For Muslims, this means looking into Islamic traditions, particularly Sufism, as a means of freeing one's internal self. Soroush recommends that Muslims look into their own long and rich past to find models of freedom seeking belief and belief seeking freedom. In searching though their own religious history, Muslims will understand that one freedom need not be sacrificed for the other. Anti-Western sentiment, and the West's ill use of external freedom, should not convince Muslims to dismiss freedom altogether.[38]

Muslims must embrace freedom despite its negative aspects. Although the ideas in a free society may challenge personal beliefs, these ideas would offend only those who are absolutist in their convictions and appreciate their own ideas more than they appreciate freedom.[39] Soroush chastises those, such as Maududi, who argue for the elimination of freedoms in an attempt to discourage provocative ideas. He criticizes believers who limit freedom in the name of religion. Such persons suffer from a lack of humility. Freedom ultimately benefits religious believers because it sustains a culture of dialogue in which different ideas can be tested until found to be true. Freedom emboldens persons to challenge the status quo and the assumptions of the establishment. Moreover, religious societies, those in which people have faith because they are free to believe, cannot help but become just societies. Just societies are free societies.

Diversity of belief reveals itself in free societies as a truth of religion and of God. Any religious community contains a plurality of beliefs, even more diverse than that demonstrated by the large numbers of religious sects and factions. "There are as many paths toward God as there are people (or even as many as people's inhalations and exhalations)," Soroush states.[40] The truth of religious plurality does not emerge in societies that discourage the freedom of conscience. A society that protects and encourages freedom of conscience accepts religious belief as both an individual and a collective experience.[41] A government that rules by *shari'a* dismisses religion as a highly personal experience for a definition of religion as solely a social institution. Although people do often freely associate with particular religious communities, the two must remain distinct if a society is to respect freedom of conscience.

## FREEDOMS, HISTORY, AND POWER

Maududi, Qutb, and Soroush agree on the necessity of freedom of conscience. They argue that freedom of conscience must be considered in relation to God, not merely in terms of permissiveness. Freedom of conscience for these three thinkers is also historically and geographically situated. Maududi and Qutb not only distance themselves from what they perceive as the immoral West but also write with the legacy of colonialism in mind. The religious arguments they make about freedom of conscience are consistent until they confront the effect of Western culture on recently colonized Muslims. When they apply their religious understanding to generate postcolonial policies, they generate problematic opportunities for Islamic governments to restrict freedom of conscience. Although Western countries may have physically removed themselves from Islamic lands, Maududi and Qutb express powerfully their fear and hatred of European culture and lingering Western values. Soroush, also critical of the West, targets his writings to the Iranian clerical system, which he believes forces people to act hypocritically in the name of religion. He addresses the issue of Western culture through the illogically restrictive attitude of Islamic clerics, who wrongly hope to erase immorality and ignorance by limiting access to Western products. Greater religiosity requires more freedom, not less. Soroush's distinction between genuine religious belief and religious jurisprudence strikes at both the government of Iran and the burden that *shari'a* has placed on Islam.[42]

Freedom of conscience has played a central role in Islamic theology and law. Writing in defense of Islam, all three scholars cite the importance of the Qur'anic verse stating that there should not be any compulsion in religion. Related to this verse are laws that permit non-Muslims, typically Jews and Christians, but also Hindus, to continue to believe and practice their faiths as they will. Maududi and Qutb apologetically write about the benevolence of Muslim rulers who enabled non-Muslims to live peacefully under their regimes, whereas non-Muslim rulers treated their subjects cruelly for having different religious traditions.[43] The tolerant rule of Muslim rulers, of course, has been the ideal and not always the practice in reality. Nonetheless, Maududi and Qutb remain aware of the persuasiveness of an Islam that has from the start respected freedom of conscience. Maududi especially expresses the need for additional freedoms related to freedom of conscience.[44] The ability to express the conscience in the form of community and discussion plays a partnership role with the freedom of conscience. For people to have the freedom to believe, but not have the freedom to express that belief, nullifies the importance of such freedoms.

Although freedom of expression is necessary to make viable freedom of conscience, the West exists as proof of freedom of expression gone awry. Maududi and Qutb see the media, crime, and sexual liberation of women as expressions that harm the conscience, rather than benefit it.[45] Even colonialism becomes an expression of the West's misguided belief in freedom. Colonialism is the perversion of external freedom, to use Soroush's phrase.[46] Without a deeper understanding of the different facets of freedom, including the freedom to submit to God's laws, humans abuse their liberties.

Where the three thinkers express differences is in the reasons for limitations on freedom of conscience. They all view the West as a poor example of freedoms of conscience and expression, but disagree over why the West has dealt with these freedoms so poorly. Maududi, like Qutb, is wary of Western culture and its divide of the spiritual life from the material life. Maududi, however, approaches the issue of freedom of conscience differently than Qutb. He does not formulate the idea of freedom of conscience as a melding of spirit and body, but rather envisions freedom of conscience as the negotiation between private and public.[47] He tries to distinguish Muslim views of private and public from Western views and uses the West as an example of how a state should not endorse freedom of conscience.

Although many of Maududi's elaborations on the idea of freedom of conscience resonate with Western law, he distinguishes Islamic views of freedom from Western ones. As in Western law, he notes the necessity of freedom of expression, association, and practice as well as the importance of privacy in relation to freedom of conscience. Maududi insists, however, that despite these similarities, the requirement that expressions of conscience be virtuous distinguishes Islamic perspectives on freedom of conscience.[48] Muslims should be allowed to practice their religion in a free society, and this means that Muslims should be allowed to promote the good and forbid the evil. In Western societies, free expression that promotes vices also prevents Muslims from carrying out religious injunctions. Moreover, these expressions are so overwhelming that Muslims have little choice but to be affected by them. Carrying out the religious injunction to promote good and forbid evil becomes impossible against such a ubiquitous power as Western culture. In upholding freedom of conscience and freedom of expression, the West has ironically curbed religious freedom for Muslims. The line that separates freedom of expression for all from the Muslim obligation to promote virtue is a blurry one that Maududi unfortunately does not elaborate on, except to provide Western culture as a warning.

For Qutb, the lack of integration of the body and soul, particularly with the freedoms of capitalistic society, enables people to seek pleasures of the body without consideration of the needs of the soul.[49] In capitalistic societies material goods and the body function as the media of commerce. Well aware of the truism that "sex sells," Qutb observes that the media exploits sexuality in the effort to reap profits and gain market share. Capitalism does not consider immoral the transgression of the body for financial gain. Both the body and the soul are corrupted.

Although communism and Christianity do not abuse freedom of expression as capitalism does, they do not fully consider the relationship of the body to the mind as it pertains to freedom of conscience. Communism and Christianity provide a false understanding of freedom of conscience. The conscience cannot be truly free if the body is neglected because the mind and the body work in tandem. The truth of this observation emerges starkly in cases of poverty. As in his discourses on democracy, Qutb demonstrates how the absence of basic material goods results in the devastation of not only bodily health but also spiritual and emotional health.[50] The conscience is no longer free, but instead enslaved to physical needs. People who lack basic material goods do not live in a state that enables them to attend freely to their conscience. Islam, unlike the ideological options available in the West, provides a unity of spirit and body that is necessary for freedom of conscience to flourish. This means not only providing for the material well-being of people but also making available an environment free of influences that disrupt the balance between spirit and body. He therefore recommends the avoidance, if not outright removal, of Western culture from Muslim life.[51]

Soroush moves beyond Maududi to resolve the tension that occurs between freedom of expression, which complements freedom of conscience, and the harms that arise with such freedom. He produces the dichotomy of internal and external freedom to understand how the West mishandles freedom of conscience.[52] Freedom of conscience consists of an internal aspect, which he defines as submission to God and the teachings of the prophets, as well as an external aspect, which covers expressions of internal thoughts and beliefs. People in the West concern themselves more with preserving external freedom, such as the right to free speech, than with nurturing internal freedom. As with Maududi and Qutb, Soroush uses the West as an example of freedom of expression irresponsibly used. Soroush, who writes later than Maududi and Qutb, witnesses even more so the overwhelming use of sex and violence in Western, especially American, media.

Although Soroush agrees with Maududi and Qutb that people can easily abuse freedom of expression, he remains much more optimistic than they do concerning the benefits of freedom. Moreover, Soroush believes that freedom of expression, even when misused, is necessary for faith, whereas Maududi and Qutb support suppression of Western arts and literature in order to encourage faith.[53] These opposing views on the issue of freedom of conscience and expression result from different approaches to the acquisition of knowledge. The stark contrast between Soroush and Qutb on the distinction between scientific and cultural knowledge could not be clearer.

Soroush's main concern about religious law is that people are forced into a hypocritical act of submission when the state endorses one kind of religious tradition over others. Speaking from the Iranian context, Soroush observes that even citizens who do not have faith in the Islamic tradition, or who believe in a form of Islam that the state does not approve, go through the motions of appropriately faithful citizens because they fear the consequences of displaying publicly their differences from the state.[54] For Soroush, the suppression of freedom of expression results not in a true religiosity but in a charade. Moreover, the restrictions on freedom prevent the nation from becoming genuinely religious. A citizenry that is authentically religious submits to religion freely, not as a result of legal rule or fear of punishment.

In direct contrast to Maududi and Qutb, Soroush believes that when a government suppresses ideas that come from other cultures, it prevents its people from discovering truths that are inseparable from religious truth. Ways of discovering the truth, of knowing God, cannot be limited to a single tradition or academic discipline. Freedom of conscience means that there are many paths to God; Islam, and certainly not one sect within Islam, is not the only means to this truth. Western contributions to the humanities and social sciences, as with the hard sciences, add to human understandings of truth, religion, and God. Simply because art or literature comes from the West does not disqualify it from contributing to the religiosity of Muslims. For Soroush all sources of knowledge contribute to faith.

As with the issue of toleration, Soroush here differs from Maududi and Qutb. Maududi and Qutb deeply distrust optimistic attitudes toward the incorporation of Western knowledge in their countries. Soroush, of course, considers such optimism proof of faith in God. The differences in their theologies stem not only from the differences in the ethical roots of their ideas but also from their unique historical perspectives. As discussed in relation to democracy and the West, Maududi and Qutb appear to borrow heavily from Ash'arite schools of Islam, whereas Soroush calls for a reexamination of philosophy's contributions to knowledge about God.[55] This suggests that Maududi and Qutb believe that Islamic traditional sources provide all that is necessary for faith and knowledge of God. Soroush, on the other hand, believes that the Qur'an, *sunna*, and *hadith*, although important, constitute but a few of the many ways in which the human mind can know God.

As theologians, Maududi, Qutb, and Soroush rely on the writings and thoughts of religious thinkers before them. Nevertheless, as historically situated humans, who aim to address the needs of their audiences, their writings reveal much about the contemporary history and politics of their native countries. The skepticism of Maududi and Qutb reflect to an extent the powerlessness of Egyptians and Muslim Indians and Pakistanis during the early and mid-twentieth century. Under the reign of Western rule and exploited for their geography and natural resources, the hardened attitudes of Muslims in their homelands find voice through Maududi and Qutb. Their pessimism and reluctance to embrace the West in any form, although extreme, arise out of their lived experience. In addition to the impact the West has had on their own peoples, Maududi and Qutb witnessed the effects of colonization and then decolonization on Muslims around the globe. The historical context of their commentaries is the primary impetus behind their strategies to distance themselves from the West and to proclaim the superiority of Islam.

By contrast, Iranians, though they certainly suffered at the hands of imperialists, were periodically able to shake off the reigns of the Western colonizers.[56] In part due to their geographic position, which was not strategically important to America until after the Second World War, in part due to more pressing distractions for the Soviets and British, and in part due to the historical momentum of successful uprisings against colonizers, Iranians endured a less consistently oppressive Western legacy of imperialism. The stunning takeover of the American embassy in Iran during the Islamic Revolution of 1978–1979 undoubtedly shifted the balance of power between Westerners and Iranians in favor of the latter. This recalibration of power, at least psychologically, did not occur to a comparable extent in the cases of the Egyptians or the Muslim Indians and Pakistanis. Because Soroush writes later than Maududi and Qutb, he also benefits from the mollifying effects of time. Several decades passed between the height of Maududi's and Qutb's influence and the current decade during which Soroush appears only to be hitting his stride. His greatest impact may yet follow.

These conjectures should not constitute a blanket statement about Pakistani, Egyptian, or Iranian scholars. There exist subcontinental and Egyptian Muslim scholars who hold very different views in comparison to Maududi and Qutb. These more liberal thinkers, who share Maududi's and Qutb's national histories, nonetheless offer a more open attitude toward Western culture and understand freedom of conscience as requiring openness to non-Muslim views.[57] In Iran, the most prominent religious scholars, including the clerics who dominate the political situation, hold views about the West and freedom of conscience that differ dramatically from those of Soroush. Soroush writes critically about the powerful, arguably majority, voice in Iran. His peers often do not share his religious views.

Although these caveats are intended to prevent a gross generalization about Islamic scholars, they should not eliminate entirely the necessity to situate scholars in their historical and political frameworks. Maududi, Qutb, and Soroush agree implicitly that they share a responsibility to speak to Muslims—and perhaps non-Muslims—about their contemporary situations. They take seriously their own ideas about the integration of the material and the spiritual and so speak to the economic, physical, and political needs of their audiences. As committed as they are to the timelessness of certain religious truths, they also understand as necessary the interpretation of Islamic texts and ideas to meet the demands of the current day.

# —5—

# Toleration . . . and Its Limits

The concept of toleration underlies the project of the Universal Declaration of Human Rights. Given the disagreements that inevitably arise when persons of different worldviews engage in dialogue over the details of human flourishing, they agree to accept some differences among them in order to create a universally acceptable set of norms. Questions may also arise regarding the extent to which one may tolerate differences without compromising one's own values. Acts of toleration, which can be practiced in different ways, as well as the attitude of tolerance, which assumes multiple forms, are subject matters ripe for interreligious and cross-cultural conversation.[1]

As with democracy and freedom of conscience, the idea of toleration has attained universal standing. Necessary for the stability of free and diverse communities, the practice of tolerating difference emerged historically centuries before the establishment of democratic governments. In the case of Islam, various Qur'anic verses and Prophetic traditions suggest toleration as the assumed norm to be violated only if necessary.

Maududi, Qutb, and Soroush view toleration through the lens of Islam. Although all agree that Islam provides resources in support of toleration, Maududi and Qutb also present arguments in favor of the limitations of toleration. These limitations complicate, though not necessarily eradicate, toleration as a universal human right. Because their restrictions on toleration arise primarily as a reaction to remedy the ills of colonialism, rather than out of purely religious reasons, contributions from Islam to a global consensus on human rights are still possible.

This chapter will not recount the successes and failures of Muslims with regard to toleration and tolerance but rather the ways in which Maududi, Qutb, and Soroush as contemporary Islamic thinkers interpret their religious tradition in order to explain the role of toleration and the principles behind it in these modern times. They also draw on historical figures and texts to make their points, but they focus primarily on presenting a religious view of the principle of toleration that is consistent with their understanding of Islam.

Although many of these thinkers' ideas about the practice of toleration, including its limits, arise in their discussions about toleration specifically, they also emerge in essays about knowledge and information, philosophy, and religion. In these passages, they refer implicitly to the limits of their tolerance. Their methods of inquiry and attitudes toward the West reveal as much about their individual views on toleration as the substance of their arguments. The complex arguments Maududi, Qutb, and Soroush offer about toleration both defy and adhere to the categorization of Islamic scholars as either liberal and intellectual or fundamentalist and conservative. Moreover, although they at times agree about the practice of toleration, their language also indicates different levels of tolerance, particularly toward Europe and the United States. Their comments on toleration, as with their comments on freedom of conscience, reveal the tension between support of these rights and protection against Western cultural imperialism. The similarities and differences among these thinkers attest once again to the complex range of thought among Islamic thinkers on values essential to universal human rights.

## TOLERATION AND DIVISION

Maududi supports, with major exceptions, the belief that Islam requires all persons to be tolerated regardless of race, ethnicity, class, or gender. Unlike Qutb or Soroush, however, he addresses the problem of intra-Muslim division and intolerance, particularly on the subcontinent, where caste differences based in Hinduism persist even among self-professed Muslims. Although Maududi is concerned about increasing the levels of tolerance within the Muslim community, he believes that too much tolerance exists for corrupt Western values. He argues that distinctions should be drawn between Muslim and Western values. Western civilization, he claims, destroys Islamic values and should not be tolerated.

Within an Islamic state such as Pakistan, Maududi asserts, every Muslim should be allowed to hold official government positions without discrimination on the basis of "race, colour, or class." Also, in such a state, both men and women, so long as they claim to support the constitution, should be allowed to vote. Furthermore, with respect to civil and criminal law, no distinction should be made between Muslims and non-Muslims.[2]

Because of his location in Pakistan and the large number of Hindus there, who are technically not Peoples of the Book, Maududi takes into account special considerations for expanding toleration to followers of non-Abrahamic traditions. He is careful to use the phrase "non-Muslims" when describing citizens of a state who are not Muslims. *Dhimmis,* who are typically assumed to be Christians or Jews under the rule of a Muslim authority, include Hindus in Maududi's writings.[3] The picture that Maududi portrays of his Muslim state is that all persons are entitled to the basic rights of a democracy.

Although all persons, even non-Muslims, should be treated equitably in an Islamic democracy, Maududi observes that Muslims discriminate against each other on the basis of caste and ethnic distinctions. He lectures to a Muslim audience in the Punjab region of India that Islam eliminates distinctions among the "Rajputs, Gakhars, Mughuls, Jats and many others" and that Muslims should stop insisting on the importance of these differences among themselves. Maududi chastises his audience for choosing not to intermarry between castes and ethnicities and for acknowledging only in theory, not in practice, the idea of Muslim brotherhood.[4] Moreover, Maududi notes that Muslims continue to practice Hindu rituals, which Islam condemns. His listeners have failed both to embrace in their actual lives the principles of Islam and to eliminate traditions that emerge out of Hindu custom. The caste system, which divides Hindu society into distinct strata, continues to exist even among Muslims who claim to have left behind other religious beliefs. Also, regional differences persist that override the idea of a single and unified community of Muslims. Muslims on the Indian subcontinent appear to marry within traditionally accepted castes and regions rather than as Muslims and across these divisions.

Muslims, although continuing to tolerate and even practice Hindu traditions, appear not to tolerate acceptable differences among each other concerning the various schools of legal thought within Islam. Several schools of jurisprudence emerged in the centuries following the advent of Islam. These schools, such as the Hanafi, Hanbali, Jafari, Maliki, and Shafi'i, represent different approaches to the interpretation of divine literature for juridical purposes. *Shari'a,* for instance, developed along the lines of these schools. Legal scholars received training in and developed preferences among these schools, and this variation was considered acceptable in the scholarly community. The differences among the schools tended to reflect differences in procedural matters and laws rather than fundamental theological principles.[5] Given the nature of these differences, Muslims, according to Maududi, should tolerate and accept those who support one school over another. With regard to these diverse schools of legal theory, so long as one believes in the divine status of the *shari'a*, one should be considered a Muslim. Maududi even reinforces the notion that Muslims have a right to understand the *shari'a* in whichever way they best see fit: "If ten Muslims follow ten different methods, all of them are surely Muslims as long as they believe that they must submit to the law of God."[6]

Although Muslims may disagree with each other about the different legal schools, they should not pass judgment as to who can claim to be Muslim. Maududi draws a clear line, however, between differences that should be tolerated and those that should not. Just as he condemns Muslims who continue to practice Hindu marriage customs by marrying along caste lines, he argues against newly converted Muslims who occasionally eat pork. When he reads a letter from a young Muslim who has traveled to China, he disagrees with the attitude of leniency toward new converts who continue to practice their local culinary traditions even when forbidden by Islam. The newly converted Chinese Muslims, the letter writer explains sympathetically, eat pork, as that is a part of their cultural cuisine. Maududi, however, finds this kind of tolerance unacceptable. He notes that the Qur'an has explicitly condemned the eating of pork. Fearing a slippery slope, he argues that if Muslims accommodate practices for reasons of subjective taste, then they can make arguments for the permissibility of activities such as gambling and drinking liquor.[7] Muslim law, in other words, should not be changed for reasons of cultural predilection or tradition. Maududi fears that the permissiveness of other cultural practices and beliefs will adulterate Muslim values.

Western-style education further facilitates the loosening of Muslim values.[8] Younger generations of Muslims learn English in schools and colleges and they neglect Arabic, the religious language of Islam, as well as their own non-Western languages and literatures. While in school, students become accustomed and ingrained to Western ways of thinking, and their opinions become informed by Western standards. Maududi believes that Western education shares little, if anything, in common with Islamic values and Muslim culture, and, as a result, students lose their Muslim identities.[9] This loss occurs not merely from the absence of Islamic education but from the inculcation of Western values.

In contrast to the Islamic civilization, Western civilization stands on a foundation not of rationality but of "feelings, lust, and urges." Maududi claims that the Western Renaissance, the source of contemporary Western values, rejected "rational guidance, logical reasoning, and innate intuition" and focused almost entirely on material results.[10] He explains that young Muslims who absorb Western ways of thinking fail to grasp the proper attitude and values of the faithful Muslim. Muslims should obey unwaveringly the authority of the Qur'an. For Maududi, to criticize the Qur'an as a Muslim is both unjust and irrational. The principles, laws, and authority of the Qur'an should not be critiqued, and to do so would be the equivalent of revoking one's identity as a Muslim. A person who claims to be Muslim, and yet criticizes the Qur'an's contents, leads a paradoxical existence.[11]

Despite his low threshold for apostasy, Maududi nonetheless concedes that one can interpret the Qur'an from different perspectives, ranging from liberal to orthodox. The common factor that ties these different Muslims, however, is the expectation to defer to the Qur'an, Islamic principles, and the *shari'a.* On this point, Maududi is adamant. To be a Muslim means to submit to God, to accept Muhammad as the Prophet, and, moreover, to surrender to the injunctions indicated in religious law. Equally important, the Muslim, if faithful, has conceded the right to demand rational proof for *shari'a.*[12]

Maududi attempts to maintain several contradictory positions on the role of rationality with regard to religion. On the one hand, he claims that Western culture is immoral due to its lack of rationality, whereas on the other hand, he argues that rationality must be limited concerning questions of faith. To add to the confusion, Maududi claims that "reason and wisdom" reveal who is a true Muslim and who is not. One way to resolve these contradictory positions is for Maududi to argue that rationality has its proper purpose in matters of ethics and religion. Outside of Islamic scripture, one applies rationality as a skeptic, carefully judging that which is morally sound or unsound. One may also appropriately adopt an attitude of skeptical rationalism prior to conversion to Islam, presumably because at that point one is not yet a Muslim. If one does not find the justification one needs to submit to God as a Muslim, then one is not required to submit to Islam, nor should Islam be imposed on the unbeliever. Once one has submitted to Islam, however, rationality should be used only to confirm the wisdom of the Islamic teachings, not to convince oneself of the benefits of belief. For Maududi, intellectual dissatisfaction does not provide sufficient rationale for refusing to obey Islamic law. To reject *shari'a* for this reason would be tantamount to denying the authority of the Prophet. Had Muhammad been required to provide rational justification for each aspect of the law, Maududi explains, Islam would never have come into being. The very existence of Islam required faithful submission to God and to the Prophet, not endless questioning and rationalizing.[13]

This threshold between belief and disbelief marks boundaries between acceptable and unacceptable intellectual arguments concerning Islam. One can differ with the Qur'an, but only after one has denounced the Islamic faith. Because disagreeing with the Qur'an, for Maududi, indicates a lack of belief in God and the Prophet, one can only do so as a non-Muslim. Non-Muslims, because they do not claim to believe in the divinity of the Qur'an, may critique without restriction the principles, rules, and ideas found in the text. A non-Muslim, however, relinquishes any right to claim to be a Muslim and to explain to Muslims the meaning of Islam. Even a well-intentioned non-Muslim may not offer suggestions as to how to promote the Islamic faith.[14] There are differences between the privileges of the believer and the nonbeliever with regard to the laws and ideas of Islam.

These stringent delineations limit creative interpretation and application of divine scripture. Although non-Muslims may exercise critical reasoning in attempts to understand the Qur'an, *hadith*, and *shari'a*, the fruits of their labors are ultimately of little or no consequence. The teachings of Islam are lost to non-Muslims. Moreover, Muslims may apply their rational capacities only to the extent that they glorify the unchanging perfection of divine texts and never question the wisdom of injunctions. Their efforts may lead only to the continuance of a frozen tradition, not to new ways of understanding the Qur'an, *sunna*, *hadith*, or *shari'a*. According to Maududi's scheme, there is no possibility for *ijtihad*, or the independent struggle to find meaning in scripture. Those who are free to perform such exegesis, the non-Muslims, are merely engaging in inconsequential intellectual games. Muslims who attempt *ijtihad* are no longer Muslims, and so their efforts become meaningless for Muslims.

Maududi's tolerance for variety within Islam is incoherently restrictive. Although he argues for toleration among Muslims, from liberal to orthodox and among the various legal schools, he also advocates an unquestioning attitude toward the Qur'an and *shari'a* as a minimum threshold of belief for any Muslim. Muslims, regardless of their political and intellectual leanings, must not exercise their God-given rational capacity to examine the authority, justness, or applicability of these texts.

Maududi's tolerance for non-Muslims wavers between apathy and spite. He does not call for the elimination of persons and things non-Muslim, yet he also does not affirm or appreciate other cultures, except when these other cultures are in conflict with the West. Unsurprisingly, Maududi does not attempt to address the issue of a multicultural citizenry within an Islamic state from the perspective of the non-Muslim. Given his responses to Hindu marriage customs and Chinese cuisine, he would likely limit other traditional customs of Muslims from various cultural and ethnic backgrounds. Because he believes that the divine texts of Islam provide all that is necessary to live, an argument for the elimination of these non-Muslim cultural practices would be in line with Maududi's thought. An Islamic state, in his opinion, must be grounded in the principles and injunctions of the Qur'an.[15] These cultural practices would presumably be replaced by Muslim duties articulated in the Qur'an and *shari'a.* In such a case, Islam ironically becomes as much a *cultural identity* as a religion.[16] Maududi's positions on toleration ultimately conflict with each other.

## THE BOUNDARIES OF TOLERATION

Both before and during the Inquisition, several Islamic rulers were known for their toleration. Even when religious persecution was rampant, Islamic leaders, most notably Salah al-Din, extended protection to non-Muslims. Despite the comparative justness of such rulers, religious violence in the name of Islam nonetheless occurred. In defense of Islam, Qutb offers an apologetic history that attests to an unblemished legacy of toleration and dismisses any barbarism on the part of "true" Muslims. He compares Islam to Christianity in particular and claims that Muslims have never persecuted as the Christians did during the Inquisition. Those moments in Islamic history when rulers committed acts of violence, Qutb claims, were done out of political necessity and were perpetrated by Muslim converts, who failed to understand their adopted religion. Islamic conquests likewise were not the result of intolerance of other people's beliefs but rather the result of the intolerance of Islam by other rulers. Non-Islamic rulers refused to allow their people to accept Islam. The wars were a means of removing obstacles set up by people who refused to allow Muslims to practice their faith. Muslims have a duty to wage war against polytheists and unbelievers. In contrast to Islamic forms of governance, "man-made" and "self-devised" systems of human organization often present obstacles to Islam and therefore present legitimate reasons for deploying physical force against them.[17] As such, Muslims are allowed to fight these opponents in order that people may have the freedom to receive Islam. Muslim rulers, however, allowed conquered peoples to choose not to adopt Islam. Rather than persecute them for their faith, the rulers imposed a poll tax.

The poll tax, according to Qutb's apologetic explanation, gave the non-Muslims "full human rights" and symbolized the tolerance of Islam. When people refused to pay poll taxes even after given the opportunity to convert to Islam, they must have been incorrigibly materialistic and incapable of incorporating Islam into their lives. The only option for dealing with such people was domination through physical force.[18] The unbelievers should be the target of violent *jihad* and treated harshly. Qutb turns to the example of the Prophet, who waged war against polytheists but gave them the opportunity to convert if they were not already *ahl al-kitab,* or People of the Book. Islamic rulers, unlike other rulers of the time, offered people options rather than straightforward persecution. If, however, people did not recognize Islam minimally as a just form of government, they were subjected to the sword. Muslims were to wage an intellectual and emotional *jihad* with the converts, and even to act harshly toward them if necessary, to spread the message of God.[19] For those who appeared to declare faith in Islam simply to avoid persecution, Qutb concedes that faithful Muslims were commanded to accept their claims of conversion and leave God to determine their true intentions.

On the issue of toleration, Qutb compares Islamic societies to the contemporary Western, specifically Christian, world and determines that Islam is the more tolerant of the two. He points out the injustice that characterizes the treatment of Native Americans by "the white man," as well as the treatment of Africans by the whites of apartheid South Africa. He blames the governments of the United States and South Africa for rejecting the divine justice of Islam. In contrast to these immoral political powers, Islam asks its believers to practice an impartial justice that is not determined by emotion or affinity. Rather, within the *umma*, all believers are equal with no distinction according to class, wealth, or influence. Islam has achieved a level of equity that has not been matched by any Western government. The justice of Islam, which asks its believers to accept each other regardless of differences, depends on obedience to God and the Prophet. Because Islam requires that people extricate themselves from servitude to others and dedicate themselves solely to God, both racial and national differences have no meaning in Islam.[20]

Qutb argues that Islam surpasses Christianity with regard not only to its history of toleration but also to the spirit of toleration embedded in the religion itself. Toleration exists in Islam more so than in the other Abrahamic religions because it asks that people look at the world around them and witness the entirety and variety of God's creation. Islam does not demand faith in miracles; instead, it insists on human rationality and the powers of observation.[21] Quoting the Qur'an, Qutb shows that God endowed humans with rationality and that God desires for humans to observe the diversity of the human race.[22] Noting the variety of languages and people, Qutb explains that these differences are marks of God's existence.[23] As signs of God's creation, the variations found among humans should be respected. Toleration as an Islamic value thus emerges out of an appreciation and understanding of God's role in creation and humanity.

The value of tolerance does not extend to all areas of life. Qutb places limits on what he accepts as valid knowledge, particularly humanistic knowledge. Although Muslims may safely acquire knowledge of the physical world from non-Muslims, they should avoid non-Muslim studies in the following disciplines: "Philosophy, interpretation of human history, Psychology (with the exception of those observations and disputed opinions that do not investigate the interpretation and explanation), Ethics, Religions and their comparative study, Social Sciences and Humanities (leaving observations, statistics and directly acquired information, and the fundamental concepts that are developed on their basis), the collective aspect and objective of all these learnings, past and present, in every period."[24] Qutb considers these areas of knowledge tainted by *jahili* beliefs, or the beliefs of those ignorant of the true nature of God.[25] The social sciences and humanities potentially corrupt Muslims through their ungodly interpretation of events and objects. By using the term *jahili* to describe these areas of study, Qutb not only indicates that these subjects are the product of non-Muslims, particularly Westerners, but also invokes the historical use of the term, which refers to the time prior to Muhammad's revelation, the *jahiliyyah.* Before the advent of Islam, people were ignorant of God and of the knowledge imparted by God through the Prophet Muhammad. Because non-Muslims fail to understand the relationship of their acquired knowledge to God, they are the equivalent of the people born before Islam. The objects of *jahili* thinking would be the equivalent of the thoughts of the ignorant.

Qutb, however, seems to believe that scientific and statistical data are objective and not easily subject to misinterpretation. The sciences, which objectively uncover the laws of nature and the universe, help to prove God's existence. As such, disciplines in the hard sciences, such as astronomy, biology, physics, and chemistry, do not contain the potential for immorality found in the humanities and social sciences. The West, despite its scientific achievements, expresses deviant desires in its non-scientific studies. Thus, although Qutb acknowledges that Muslims in present times learn about the hard sciences from Western institutions and sources, he urges extreme caution in accepting such information.

Muslims must carefully separate non-Muslims' "abstract learnings" about the world from their interpretations of those facts. The slightest Western influence, he warns, would contaminate the purity of their Islamic beliefs.[26]

Qutb does not suggest that Muslims completely avoid the research and studies of non-Muslims. This is not because Qutb believes that non-Muslims occasionally provide reliable information, however. On the basis of his personal experience as well as his interpretation of divine texts, Qutb asserts that Jews and Christians produce only poor research. If Muslims encounter the interpretive and humanistic scholarship of non-Muslims, they should not do so with the intent to understand the subject matter. Rather, Muslims should view their encounters with "*jahili* research" as opportunities to reaffirm the inadequacies and falsehoods of the ignorant. This research might also offer opportunities for determining how to eliminate such ignorance and to convert those who have yet to embrace the Islamic life and faith.[27]

To prove his point, Qutb applies Qur'anic verses and *hadith* to convince his readers that the People of the Book lack good intentions. In these passages, God warns Muslims that Jews and Christians will attempt to lure them away from the straight path because they themselves are misguided. Upon the basis of these selections, Qutb categorically denounces any insight offered by Jews and Christians on any aspect of Islam. He asserts that a Muslim who extends goodwill to the People of the Book suffer from lack of reason and intellect. Even if Jews and Christians discuss with good intention and the utmost sincerity any aspect of Muslim life, including politics, society, and the economy, they must not be trusted. Muslims must also avoid Jews and Christians who seek knowledge from Muslims about Islam. Qutb admonishes those Muslims who encourage this type of exchange because they are violating the word of God.[28]

This refusal to learn from non-Muslim sources presents one of many of Qutb's inconsistent claims concerning toleration in the Islamic traditions. Although he praises Islam for its historical toleration of Jews and Christians, he also believes that Muslims may justly persecute people whom he believes present an ungodly opposition to Islam. He believes that *jihad* should be waged in its intellectual and emotional form against hypocrites, and even in its physical form against unbelievers. He maintains that Muslims should read Western literature and research but only to seek scientific knowledge, not humanistic knowledge. Qutb attempts to draw lines between the universal, the evil West, and Islam. Muslims and Westerners share scientific knowledge, which is universal and divine. Scientific knowledge of God's creation would be the same regardless of its source, and, moreover, it represents God's influence on earth. Qutb argues that interpretive knowledge from the West, however, would taint the purity of Islam. Although he appears to soften in the presence of great Western literature, Qutb claims that humanistic and social scientific work from the West threatens Islamic values.

As with the issue of democracy and equality, Qutb wants Muslims to express their identity independent of the West. He does so by bolstering Islam through an apologetic history and explanations of the values espoused by Islam. He quotes extensively from the Qur'an and *hadith* literature to show that certain themes, especially justice, appear from the beginning of Islam. Nonetheless, when he provides Muslims with strategies to reduce the excessive influence of Western culture and to revive Islamic traditions, he contradicts his own assertions regarding the divine nature of diversity. He tries, but ultimately fails, to make simultaneous arguments for and against toleration.

## TOLERATING FREEDOM

Given his belief in the unity of truth, Soroush predictably maintains the necessity of religious toleration in societies claiming to uphold human rights. He argues consistently that a plurality of voices, both secular and religious, is required in order for justice to prevail. Moreover, a religious person who is intolerant of other persons due to their beliefs commits an intellectual error in failing to distinguish between people and beliefs. One may disagree with a belief and find it false, yet at the same time find the bearer of that belief "blameless, respectable, and even commendable." One should tolerate people, even if one finds their ideas intolerable.[29] In order to arrive at the truth, one needs to consider multiple ideas, regardless of the religious identity of the person expressing them.

Soroush argues that certain global concerns, such as world peace, human rights, women's rights, and the environment, require the input of multiple faith traditions. "We are all travelers on a ship," he analogizes, "if one person pokes a hole in it, all of us will drown." Although these issues may have originated as nonreligious concerns, the impact, pervasiveness, and ubiquity of these problems have left their mark on religious thought and dialogue. The concept of human rights may have been created initially by secular philosophers and expounded on by political thinkers, but it has become an unavoidable aspect of contemporary religious thought. Religions today that do not promote human rights, that are not fundamentally just, cannot thrive. Moreover, religious knowledge, insofar as it contributes to general knowledge, can contribute positively to our understanding of these concerns. Dialogue across disciplines, cultures, and faiths may ameliorate global problems. Muslims should take advantage of the technology available today to participate in interfaith and global dialogues concerning issues of universal importance. Technology has made it possible to engage in research about other traditions, including Christianity and Judaism, and as a result, interfaith dialogues with the goal of sharing solutions and reconciling differences are feasible. Although some problems remain local, those that are global in scope deserve universal, shared consideration.[30]

By seeking religious knowledge across traditions, one enjoys a bounty of ideas that may benefit global concerns. God's guidance, after all, is wide-reaching and not limited to a particular faith. One's own faith need not interfere with the appreciation of another's faith tradition. Soroush compares, for example, the lives of Mohammad al-Ghazzali (1058–1111) and Saint Francis of Assisi (1182–1226), both of whom, he claims, are "praise-worthy" and "honorable," although each man lived in a different place, time, and context. Despite their differences, both persons toiled assiduously in their search for God, and their insights benefit all.[31]

Religious toleration results not from "'liberal-mindedness,' faithlessness, or skepticism." Rather, it stems from a profound understanding of human nature and an appreciation of and familiarity with the "intricacies of the human soul."[32] The cause of one's belief or disbelief is, according to Soroush, a result of a preordained heavenly cause. One may have various reasons for believing in a particular faith and the free will to practice that faith, but why a person believes in one faith over another or believes in a faith at all is due to divine causes beyond the legislation of humans. Because the cause of religious belief is divine, humans would err to suppress its existence in its various forms.

Believers of different faith traditions often claim that theirs is the only path to salvation and that therefore they should not tolerate people's beliefs in other traditions. They may attempt to proselytize others or to label them as infidels and wage war against them. The presence of multiple expressions of faith and different perspectives, however, leads Soroush to believe that perhaps God favors religious pluralism and diversity. Like Maududi and Qutb, he uses the human powers of rationality and observation to remark on the diversity found among humans. Unlike his predecessors, however, Soroush affirms that each of these religious traditions may offer an "aspect of the truth," the whole of which can only be discovered by acknowledging these insights into "guidance and salvation."[33]

Soroush studies the idea of religious toleration from the perspective of Western thinkers, including Barth, Jung, Brunner, Hick, Smart, and

Toynbee, and sees that problems on this topic persist not only in Islam but also in Christianity.[34] Theologians continue to differ regarding the possibility of revelation and salvation outside of the Christian faith. Some, such as Hick, acknowledge the truth of other religious traditions, whereas Barth and Brunner do not. Soroush admires the Catholic Church for recognizing paths to salvation outside of the church, including Islam, and hopes that Muslims, too, can come to accept the truth of other perspectives of God, both among Muslims themselves and among non-Muslims. Many Muslims have forgotten the implications of the Qur'anic verse advising "no compulsion in religion." In the case of religious faith, one must not fault others for believing differently. Here Soroush pushes the exegesis further and reasons that if multiple faiths emerge not out of human compulsion but from divine cause, then religious pluralism should be embraced as divine.

Religious pluralism presents an argument in favor of religious democracy. In keeping with his definition of democracy as a method of restraining power, Soroush argues that the "only thing that is required of a democracy is tolerance of different points of view and their advocates." The presence of multiple points of view, through channels such as the free press and multiple political parties, serves to check excesses of power. The free expression of alternative religious views is particularly important in religious governments, but it is also important in secular ones because belief contributes to diversity. Because belief takes on multiple forms, it is far more diverse than disbelief. If secular governments wish to uphold diversity and pluralism, then they must accommodate religious communities. The presence of multiple faiths and multiple understandings of religion contributes to a refined understanding of the complex principles of justice and rights.[35]

In democratic countries that are governed by religious law, allowing for free expression of faith enables religious democracy to create "free, just and reasonable" religious jurisprudence. The problem with many Islamic governments today is the monolithic view that incorrectly equates religious law (*shari'a*) with religion and religious government. Religious law is not the same as the religion of Islam, nor is it the whole of religious government. This false view of religion and jurisprudence would presumably be corrected by the toleration and consideration of alternate views on Islam. "Free faith and dynamic religious understanding are inseparable from free, just, and reasonable jurisprudence," Soroush argues. Where religious law can be free, just, and reasonable through open discourse, "religious jurisprudence will be more effective than a secular jurisprudence" in a society consisting of religious and faithful citizens.[36]

Soroush's method of religious reasoning, which consists in seeking truth tolerant of all disciplines, mimics the process he recommends for a religious democracy. Truths everywhere are compatible with each other regardless of where they are located geographically or in time. His personal experience of the Islamic Revolution created in him the desire to collect truths related to the event to solve the problems, both theoretical and practical, of the late 1970s that continue to the present.[37] One major problem with the Islamic government of Iran is that it has avoided building a theoretical basis for its existence as a religious democracy, requiring it to examine extra-Qur'anic sources of knowledge. Relying solely on their interpretation of the Qur'an and religious sources such as *hadith* and *sunna*, however, Iranian clerics recklessly attempt to guide their nation into an age when the adoption and reconciliation of ideas from outside the Qur'an have become both evident and necessary. A government today must, for example, acknowledge the truth behind the concept of human rights, despite its extrareligious origins. Soroush argues that the idea of revolution is itself extrareligious and not originally Islamic, yet it was an idea adopted successfully by Iran's clerical leaders.[38]

In a search for truth not unlike Soroush's methodology, the leaders of an Islamic government today must look beyond themselves to enrich its current environment, which is intellectually impoverished insofar as it is lagging in theoretical knowledge from outside Islam. The society must reconsider its stagnant understanding of religious government and should "freely and deliberately" reconsider its understanding of humanity and reassess its aims and goals. Once guiding values for a religious democracy have been determined, the government must adopt a system to realize those goals. The adoption of a system of government that is rational and consistent, as well as just, is essential to democracies, including religious ones. In a religious democracy, toleration for multiple sources of truth can provide the insight necessary to develop the theoretical basis and proper method for establishing a government.[39]

Governments today need to adopt a posture toward religion like they have toward science. As a philosopher of science, Soroush understands that scientific knowledge resembles humanistic and social scientific knowledge in its historical development.[40] Science, though regarded as objective, is nevertheless a product of conversations among scientists and across time, just as other forms of knowledge are produced among scholars through history. Governments do not discriminate against scientific knowledge on the basis of its cultural, political, or ethnic source, but they still believe they should discriminate against religious knowledge for any of these reasons. They fail to see that religious knowledge must be open to the same kind of scrutiny and testing to which scientific knowledge is regularly subjected. If religions are to yield information of the quality that the sciences produce, they must flourish in a similarly free environment. Instead, religions and their study are feared and shrouded in mystery. Religious debate and scholarship are not tolerated.

Iran's religious clerics fear the negative consequences of religious toleration. By allowing any kind of religious belief and dialogue to take place, they believe, moral anarchy will ensue. Soroush turns this argument for protecting Islam on its head. To protect Islam, and the knowledge it contains, societies must endorse toleration of all faiths and beliefs, even those that appear morally corrupt. In the long run, a strategy of religious toleration is the only one that will allow Islam to flourish.

## KNOWLEDGE, DIALOGUE, AND TOLERATION

Maududi, Qutb, and Soroush understand the concept of toleration in vastly different ways. Although all agree that toleration is a principle worthy of putting into practice, their attitudes of tolerance vary significantly. On a continuum, Maududi's ideas appear the least tolerant, and Soroush's position expresses the greatest level of both tolerance and toleration. The significant differences among the three emerge in examining the compatibility of their epistemological methods, or the ways in which they seek knowledge, with their religious arguments for toleration.

The primary struggle for both Maududi and Qutb appears in their attempts to reconcile Qur'anic injunctions to tolerate the People of the Book with their perceived threats of Western culture. On the one hand, they exalt Islam for its stance toward toleration, but on the other hand they refuse to extend that toleration to anything Western. Their fear and hatred of the West cloud their ability to find value in Western culture. Instead, their praise of toleration turns into discrimination.

Maududi and Qutb invoke the ills of the West in their comparisons between Islamic and non-Islamic countries. Maududi observes, presciently, the hypermaterialism found in Western counties, and Qutb rightly points out the violent history of intolerance and prejudice in the predominantly Christian societies of the United States and South Africa.[41] They then use their observations to argue that the West is morally inferior to Islamic societies. At the time that Maududi and Qutb wrote, in the middle of the twentieth century, their arguments would have seemed quite persuasive. The United States was experiencing unprecedented postwar wealth, and consumerism was on the rise. The civil rights movement in the United States and the end of apartheid in

South Africa seemed a long way off. Indeed, even in the drafting of the Universal Declaration of Human Rights, Eleanor Roosevelt, the United States representative and head of the drafting committee, feebly defended the lack of equality between "colored people" and whites in the United States by stating only that progress was being made.[42] Although South Africa with its rule of apartheid was treated by the United Nations as an outsider even then, many countries appeared to condone its government through trade and acceptance of nations' rights to sovereignty.

One danger in Maududi's and Qutb's writings, of course, is that their anti-Western messages are read today without consideration of the historical context of these thinkers or of the changes that have happened in the last few decades with regard to civil rights and apartheid. Instead, the "spirit" of their writings continues to thrive when applied to the situation of the United States in the Middle East. Their readers not only perceive that prejudice is still alive and well in the United States; they also see the rise of American economic colonialism in the oil-rich Middle East and cultural imperialism throughout the world. The popularity of sex-laden and violent American films and television shows helps to reinforce the sentiment of Maududi and Qutb that the West is morally corrupt.

Although Maududi and Qutb appear hypocritical in praising tolerance and arguing so intolerantly against the West, they effectively persuade their audiences that the West has come to its sinful place because of its excessive permissiveness. They also argue that as victims of Western imperialism, they must be careful not to become excessively tolerant to the point of inflicting harm to themselves.[43] From their perspective, Muslims have been so tolerant that their oppressors took advantage of them and forced them into continual subservience. Tolerance, in other words, must have its limits. Muslims must not tolerate the ways in which the West tricks them into submission. Maududi and Qutb also observe, moreover, the pitfalls of too much tolerance as practiced by the citizens of the United States and the countries of Western Europe. In tolerating too much, the West has become a breeding ground for corruption. The West stands as an example of tolerance taken past its limits. Maududi and Qutb are determined to regulate tolerance so that Muslims will not become immoral like the people in the West or be taken advantage of by them.

The unfortunate situation for Muslim countries, apparent both during the time of Maududi and Qutb and continuing to this day, is that the countries these thinkers view as morally corrupt are also masters of economic and scientific progress. That the countries of the West, despite their evil natures, are wealthy and technologically advanced in comparison to Muslim countries provides an endless source of frustration. Here,

Maududi and Qutb face a question of theodicy: why does God appear to favor the evil while allowing the good to suffer? In response, Maududi claims that Muslims need to become better Muslims, such that their moral superiority will overcome the temporary material prowess of the Westerners.[44] They need to become more literal, less compromising, and more vigilant about following the Qur'an and the *shari'a.* They must at all costs abstain from any expression of Western value systems. Qutb creates a methodological distinction between types of Western knowledge that allows Muslims to seek Western scientific expertise while still condemning Western culture as expressed in literature, the humanities, and social sciences.[45] He separates scientific knowledge from cultural knowledge so that Muslims may acquire the technical information required to advance in the world economically but not expose themselves to the moral stain of the West found in the humanities and social sciences. He does not consider the fact that the hard sciences, too, are often marked by cultural prejudices.[46]

Soroush rejects Qutb's dichotomy between scientific and humanistic knowledge because he views the method of acquiring knowledge through time as the same in both cases.[47] The sciences, like the arts, develop within cultural contexts, and the conversations that transmit knowledge, whether in the humanities or in the natural sciences, are similar in structure, even if the specific vocabulary differs. If the ultimate goal in these conversations is to acquire truth, then the ideas themselves, not the carriers of knowledge, must become the valued currency.

Soroush's faith in the ultimate discovery of the "truth," however, glosses over the fear expressed by Maududi and Qutb that the exchange of knowledge is an unequal one, marred by domination. As noted in chapter 1, Habermas addresses these very concerns in his exchanges with Gadamer. Habermas argues that unequal power relations between interlocutors systematically distort the language used in dialogue. He assumes that language, knowledge, and power are proportionately related to each other, and thus when language reflects domination, it indicates disproportional ownership of both knowledge and power.[48] The imbalance of power between participants in the conversation remains. Habermas proposes that interlocutors apply social theory and Freudian psychoanalysis to understand and then treat the sources of systematic distortion. Once we understand the roots of our psychoses, we can begin the process of creating an ideal speech situation, one in which public, undistorted language transmits knowledge fairly. The consequence of remedied language is the egalitarian distribution of knowledge and power.

Gadamer responds that Habermas's understanding of society, language, and psychology comes from the culture and language that form him. Habermas himself is trapped in an epistemological circle—what he already knows determines what he will know. The recommendation of Freudian psychology in particular unleashes an entire set of concerns about domination and cultural bias. The therapy that Habermas recommends to solve the problem of domination relies on a self-defeating analogy of a therapist and patient—a clear example of imbalanced power dynamics. The suggestion that psychoanalysis can offer a cure for societies' diseases finds its basis in an unequal relationship between the healer and the ill.

Habermas nonetheless brings to the fore the need to reform language and conversation into a universal, rather than privileged, practical philosophy. Habermas, more so than Gadamer, understands that the systematic distortion of language can prevent us from even recognizing others as human beings capable of rational, interpreted experience. Gadamer assumes empathy between interlocutors, which though perhaps too optimistic, seems nonetheless accurate given the requirements of conversation.[49] Language, in other words, is not so systematically distorted that progress cannot be made. Habermas must concede this point to Gadamer. If Habermas believes that humans can create an "ideal speech situation" out of the linguistic abilities we possess, then the seeds of progress must already exist within our current conversational capacities.

Soroush's descriptions of a progression toward truth through dialogue resonate with Gadamer's process of the "fusion of horizons" that occurs between persons in conversation. According to Gadamer, when people engage in dialogue, they see each other's perspective and thereby alter their own "horizons," their lines of view. Their horizons change as their understanding of a situation changes. Their ultimate stance on a position may not change—that is not what Gadamer means by a fusion of horizons—but rather their perspective is no longer the same as it had been before the conversation. Soroush's process of coming to know the truth through dialogue is, in form, Gadamerian. Soroush differs from Gadamer, however, in his primary faith in the existence of a universal truth that is God. All fusions of horizons, for Soroush, eventually lead us to God.

Maududi and Qutb manifest the fears expressed by Habermas in his theory on systematically distorted language. The solution suggested by Maududi, Qutb, and Habermas to correct the distortion lies in their faith in uncorrupted disciplines of study. For Qutb the cure lies in the hard sciences, whereas for Habermas it is in the social sciences, namely, psychology. Qutb's dichotomy of types of knowledge appears, however, unsustainable. As Gadamer and Soroush rightly point out, the means by and the context in which information is shared, regardless of the academic discipline, influence the information exchanged. The sharing of scientific information and the process of psychotherapy take place in specific contexts that leave indelible marks on the topics discussed, as well as on the discussants themselves.

In each of these perspectives, toleration is an assumed value in dialogue. Though Maududi, Qutb, and Habermas attempt to impose structures on the way in which dialogue takes place, information exchanges do occur and, indeed, must take place in order to end domination. Their measured, guarded, and self-conscious approach to dialogue is understandable, given the history of oppression to which they are justly sensitive. Until we reach that point of achieving Habermas's ideal speech situation, however, the best we can do is to continue to tolerate each other's differences in conversation. Strictly isolationist positions, as Maududi, Qutb, and Soroush realize, are untenable in today's world. The most promising strategy for global justice demands toleration so that important conversations can take place without fear or reservation.

# CONCLUSION

# *Advancing Human Rights Dialogue*

Even though the relatively recent concept of "human rights" is not native to traditional religious texts such as the Qur'an, the pervasiveness of human rights as a subject of discussion among Islamic traditionalists suggests that even the most conservative thinkers modify their discourse to incorporate compelling extrareligious ideas. In part because Maududi, Qutb, and Soroush have accepted the relevance of human rights to Muslims and share the common subject of Islam, they are able to engage in dialogue with each other across time and space concerning the appropriate role of religion in human rights.[1] Variances in geography, history, and the Sunni and Shi'ite traditions expand the possibilities within Islam for relating to human rights. Moreover, their similarities and differences with regard to Islam help to fuel not just intra-Islamic discussions about the role of religion and human rights. Human rights have emerged as part of dialogue both within and outside of the Islamic scholarly community.

The discussions by Soroush on democracy, toleration, and human rights stand out as the most compatible with current Western notions of human rights. Although Soroush is critical of the liberties that Americans and Europeans take with regard to their freedom, he nonetheless espouses a method of seeking truth that meshes easily with Western standards of freedom. His belief that the ultimate truth is found through open discussion and consideration of multiple points of view, even those seen as derogatory toward one's own, is echoed in American First Amendment protections of freedom of speech, belief, and assembly. Soroush's openness toward religious dialogue in the public square perhaps even exceeds the limits on speech dictated by the constitutional separation of church and state in the United States. His willingness to endure the disappointments that inevitably arise with freedom encourages cross-cultural dialogue. Most important, Soroush's belief that there are many paths to God enables him to engage in a dialogue with followers of different faith traditions and to examine more generally the role that religion can play in promoting human rights. At times, internal dialogue within the Islamic tradition seems to present a more difficult political challenge for Soroush than external dialogue with non-Muslims.[2] His efforts to open up dialogue within Islam, particularly in the context of the contemporary Iranian government, have been met with much frustration.

The case for cross-cultural and interreligious dialogue becomes far more difficult with Maududi and Qutb. Although Maududi makes explicit his desire to open up dialogue within Islam, both he and Qutb take pains not to engage with the West.[3] Their efforts to restrict freedom of and access to information indicate more than an understandable lack of trust in Western culture. Given their attempts to release Muslims from the legacy of colonialism, which includes limiting exposure to the humanistic and social scientific products of the West, the prospect of dialogue with Westerners appears bleak. Nevertheless, the inconsistencies in their arguments suggest that their strategies for eliminating Western influence cannot endure in the long term. Maududi and Qutb appear to distrust the ability of Muslims to determine for themselves cultural, political, and economic boundaries. Although they argue that Islam supports democracy, freedom, and toleration, they do so with severe restrictions. In the face of their admittedly challenging perspectives, there are encouraging indicators of the possibility of conversations with the West over human rights. For all their fears of Western cultural hegemony, Maududi and Qutb have nonetheless claimed the general concept of human rights as valid within Islam. They have shown at the very least a rhetorical acceptance of the validity of human rights in a traditionalist Islamic context. They also understand Islam as a democratic tradition that demands the active pursuit of social and economic justice.

The complex and diverse views of Islam presented by Maududi, Qutb, and Soroush contradict assumptions made by such scholars as Ignatieff and Donnelly on the contributions that Islam, and religions more generally, can and should make toward human rights. Although Ignatieff and Donnelly are correct to point out the horrific ways in which religion has been used to deny people their rights, they fail to point out the numerous ways in which religion has motivated people to provide others their human rights. Civil rights, women's suffrage, abolition, health care, and literacy have all benefited from the contributions of religion. Almost needless to say, the very existence of the UDHR depended on the inclusion of religion in the discussions on human rights.

Ignatieff's concern that religion offers mainly quietist ways of dealing with human rights abuses ignores the practical ways in which religion contributes to larger efforts. In addition to providing spiritual guidance, religion motivates believers to act for justice. Religion, like politics and economics, touches on many aspects of human life. Religion does not only take place in a mosque, church, synagogue, or temple. Maududi, Qutb, and Soroush show how the life of a Muslim extends beyond ritual practice. Islam requires the struggle for just government, material equity, toleration, and respect for the conscience. Although they disagree on how these struggles should be carried out, they agree that Islam demands more than prayer.

Shue's clarification of the role of duty in human rights provides a way in which religious and nonreligious thinkers might successfully converse with each other. In pointing out that the focus on rights ignores the complementary and necessary role of duty, especially in ensuring basic rights such as subsistence, security, and freedom, Shue offers a model that adapts easily to the language of duty found in Islamic texts. The command to enjoin the good and forbid evil, which supports many of the arguments offered by Maududi and Qutb, could be used as a starting point for cross-cultural dialogue on human rights.

Discussions concerning the role of Islam in the West, particularly in such a diverse culture as the United States, have in recent years become increasingly important. The desire to understand the relationship between Islam and terrorist activity in particular has fueled people's interests in what many see as a foreign, oppressive, and violent tradition. Because public schools do not teach about religion and relatively few Americans learn about Islam through a balanced and thorough media, ignorance and uncharitable imaginations run rampant. Yet, Americans realize that religions, particularly the Abrahamic traditions, play an important role in formulating public policy. Several of the most significant policy issues today, ranging from the stabilization of Iraq to human cloning, command both political and religious attention.

Although three thinkers should not represent the faith of more than one billion Muslims living in the world today, their influence, prominence, and geographic diversity suggest that cross-cultural discourse between Islam and the liberal West is both possible and necessary. Moreover, human rights, embodied in the notions of democracy, freedom of conscience, and toleration, serve as a common subject matter for dialogue. Gadamer suggests that "to come to an understanding about the subject matter" requires both imagination and reciprocity.[4] Participants in conversation focus on and attempt to re-create the other's words, phrases, and ideas in such a way as to make sense to oneself and to come to eventual agreement on a subject matter. This process of moral imagination in dialogue is severely restrained when persons conversing about basic human rights are not encouraged to speak about religion. To come to an understanding about the subject matter of human rights requires an ethic that allows for religious expression.

Moral imagination in cross-cultural dialogue requires reciprocity.[5] In order to have a dialogue or to have a conversation, all persons involved must be willing and capable of translating the expressions of each other. Thinkers such as Maududi and Qutb recognize that Westerners for the last few centuries have not reciprocated the practice of moral imagination. Rather than view Muslims of Africa, the Middle East, and South Asia as capable of contributing to dialogue, colonialists objectified their subjects and required them to participate in civil life under foreign terms. Maududi and Qutb, while asserting an Islamic foundation for toleration, argue that for historical reasons they must not tolerate the West until Muslims recover their own voice. Soroush, as suggested by his understanding of truth, expresses concern that the silencing of non-Muslim voices confuses Islam as finite identity rather than as universal religion. Soroush asks Muslims to partake in dialogue in order to understand better the truths that Islam holds.

The attempt to understand Islamic thinkers in their diversity is to practice moral imagination. Human rights function in many ways as an ideal mediating text for discourse. A complex set of ideas, and significant in their implications, human rights, like religion, inspire passionate conversation because they speak to the most basic values of humanity. To fail to engage religion fully into our conversations about protecting human rights would be to deprive us of understanding the contributions that religion and human rights make to the other. Only in such an environment will our moral imaginations flourish.

Ignatieff validly asserts the importance of practical approaches to human rights. In his opinion, this includes careful consideration of the political and economic aspects of implementing human rights. One need not dismiss political strategies and economic support of human rights, however, in order to accommodate religious belief. Religious reasoning, including the use of religious language, provides the validation and motivation necessary for the success of practical aspects of human rights. Moreover, the absence of religious reasoning in human rights discussions adversely affects attempts to improve both understanding and tolerance. Because people unfortunately sometimes exploit religion as a justification to oppress others, religious believers who champion human rights should be afforded every opportunity to voice this alternative view of religion. A human rights policy of dismissal with regard to religious reasoning fails to acknowledge the fact of religious reasoning in public, political dialogue. With such approaches, believers of different religious traditions and nonreligious persons remain purposefully uninformed about the decision-making process of other members of their community. Rather than perpetuate ignorance, frank discussion broadens possibilities for finding common human rights goals among admittedly diverse populations. Human rights activists and thinkers should keep in mind the ways in which religious belief contributes to social justice.

Religious traditions offer resources for thinking about profound social problems. Religious beliefs and other comprehensive doctrines help to place into perspective the information provided by other forms of analysis. Religion can help to safeguard respect for the sanctity of life even when other indicators, whether statistical, economic, or otherwise, may encourage its violation. Religious beliefs also provide a basis for identifying and critiquing social ills. Movements for social equality in communities marred by racial and gender discrimination often find their origins in churches and support in religious texts. Martin Marty points out that in "the civil rights cause, the movements for women's rights, and human rights in general, as well as in debates over population and development, war and peace, the record shows that religious forces played constructive roles."[6]

The inclusion of religious voices promotes true diversity in politics. The ability to incorporate ideas and texts from a particular religious or cultural tradition into public life lends to the diversity of a community. Kathryn Tanner argues that unless participants in public debates acknowledge distinctive religious traditions, they dangerously deny the "fact of pluralism."[7] People's identities include not only ethnic and gender components but also a vast array of other distinguishing qualities that inform the ways in which we live. Religious beliefs should count as a characteristic of identity. People do not formulate opinions on matters of public debate simply by virtue of the gender, ethnicity, class, or other more commonly cited categories of identification. To ignore or suppress the multifaceted, integrative nature of a person's character would only lead to a limited understanding of human nature. When people share religious views on a matter, they give their audiences the opportunity to learn not only about their particular understanding of their faith traditions but also about the complexity of individuals. Incorporating religious views into one's understanding of persons makes stereotyping difficult and encourages people to look beyond the superficial.

Allowing persons the opportunity to present religious reasons for public, political action may prevent future harms associated with political oppression. When communities discourage free expression, including religious expression, numerous ills arise. People become discontented if their ideas cannot be expressed as they so choose. Even if a community decides not to endorse the ideas of a particular person or group, that person or group of persons has the satisfaction of knowing that they possess the opportunity to offer their ideas through sanctioned means to the public. Reasonable members of a democratic and pluralistic society understand that their ideas coexist with other ideas. With this understanding, they acknowledge that society will not endorse only their ideas all the time. They should expect, however, that they will be given the chance to present their best case possible. Although avoiding or disguising religious language in public discussion may be a politically savvy way to avoid alienating potential supporters, such tactics should be left up to the individual or the representative group to exploit. These tactics may be encouraged, but they need not be a prerequisite for participation in political dialogue.

Religious speech at times appeals to the emotions as well as to reason. Ideas in public spaces appear in multiple forms. Speech, like art or an art in itself, presents form and content as inextricable from each other. People experience the power of religious speech through not only its distinctive content but also its particular cadences, styles, and formats. The unique diction, rhythms, and imagery sometimes found in religious speech contribute to its content. The mesmerizing speeches of Martin Luther King Jr., for example, appealed to people through emotion, reason, and politics. Nonreligious speech, even if the message or ultimate goal may be similar, may not present its argument as effectively.

Such scholars as Ronald Thiemann argue that the emotional aspects of religious speech, although acceptable, should not be encouraged in the public sphere. Thiemann believes that people should be "free to offer public arguments that appeal to emotion, base instincts, and private sources of revelation, but democratic societies should encourage citizens to resist such appeals as incompatible with fundamental values of a liberal polity."[8] Although Thiemann and others understandably want to divorce emotional appeals from political decision making, they falsely label decisions based on emotions as necessarily bad. Emotion in the form of empathy, for instance, may in many situations convey more appropriately why a person stands in favor of or opposed to a particular decision. Concern for the plight of others awakens both the emotional and rational capacities of persons. Religious traditions offer various means by which to elicit concern for others and provide justifications for those concerns.

Religion should play a role in human rights discussions. It can not only contribute to our understanding of why human life and safety are inviolable but also offer practical ways to implement human rights. Religious language and reasoning are often persuasive where nonreligious language has no effect. The use of religious reasoning, particularly the use of religious language, does carry the danger of alienating some nonreligious thinkers or believers of other faith traditions. The burden in such cases lies with the users of religious language to make as clear as possible to those who do not share their worldview why they believe as they do. Although the most fundamental aspects of faith and belief may not be translatable, there are parallel concepts—especially among human rights thinkers and activists—that are similarly ineffable. Belief in the dignity of humans, the principle of justice, and the value of helping others are arguably "foundational" beliefs that are as difficult to rationalize as belief in God. Nonreligious thinkers who want to focus solely on human rights without regard to these axiomatic beliefs should nonetheless be informed of them, particularly if they insist on the universalism of human rights. They must be clear as to which aspects of human rights are universal and why they are universal in order to engage fully in human rights discussions with skeptics who view human rights as a form of Western cultural hegemony.

The works of Maududi, Qutb, and Soroush suggest that the incorporation of Islamic thought into the perpetuation of a universal human rights ethic is important. The precedent of a variety of Islamic voices in the human rights debates prior to the signing of the UDHR stands as proof of how Islam can contribute to the wide acceptance of human rights, even in territories that had been previously colonized by key members of the UN. Accepting a diversity of Islamic voices and engaging them in dialogue help to break down barriers that assume Islam's hostility to human rights. Although some interpretations of Islam, such as those posed by Maududi and Qutb, pose difficulties to American and European ideals, to dismiss those voices altogether would be to worsen the problems that plague people of diverse faiths in the name of human rights.

# NOTES

## INTRODUCTION

1. Thomas Pogge, "How Should Human Rights Be Conceived?" in *The Philosophy of Human Rights,* ed. Patrick Hayden (St. Paul, MN: Paragon, 2001), 190–92.
2. John Rawls, *Political Liberalism* (New York: Columbia University Press, 1996), 174–76, 242–43.
3. Michael Ignatieff, *Human Rights as Politics and Idolatry* (Princeton, NJ: Princeton University Press, 2001), 81–90.
4. I use the terms "Western" and "non-Western" cautiously because they set up a duality that disguises the overlapping histories and cultures of Europe, North America, the Middle East, and Southeast Asia. Also, the terms themselves presuppose that Western is the standard and that Islam represents the absence of that standard. Because the terms are so readily accessible to readers, however, I continue to use the term "Western" to identify North American and continental European thought.
5. Roxanne Euben, *Enemy in the Mirror: Islamic Fundamentalism and the Limits of Modern Rationalism: A Work of Comparative Political Theory* (Princeton, NJ: Princeton University Press, 1999), 13.
6. Charles Taylor, *Philosophy and the Human Sciences* (New York: Cambridge University Press, 1985), 116–17.
7. Taylor, *Philosophy and the Human Sciences*, 116–33.
8. David Little and Sumner B. Twiss, *Comparative Religious Ethics* (San Francisco: Harper and Row, 1978).
9. Lee Yearley, *Mencius and Aquinas: Theories of Virtue and Conceptions of Courage* (Albany: State University of New York Press, 1990), 1, 3.
10. Sumner B. Twiss and Bruce Grelle, eds., *Explorations in Global Ethics: Comparative Religious Ethics and Interreligious Dialogue* (Boulder, CO: Westview Press, 2000), 3.
11. Clifford Geertz, *The Interpretation of Cultures* (New York: Basic Books, 1973), 6–16.
12. See, for example, Paul Berman, "The Philosopher of Islamic Terror," *New York Times Magazine*, March 23, 2003.
13. Abdullahi An-Na'im, *Toward an Islamic Reformation: Civil Liberties, Human Rights, and International Law* (Syracuse, NY: Syracuse University Press, 1990); Abdullahi An-Na'im, ed., *Human Rights in Cross-Cultural Perspectives: Quest for Consensus* (Philadelphia: University of Pennsylvania

Press, 1992); Ann Elizabeth Mayer, *Islam and Human Rights: Tradition and Politics* (Boulder, CO: Westview Press, 1991).

14. See, for example, Nasr Abu Zayd, *Rethinking the Qur'an: Towards a Humanistic Hermeneutics* (Utrecht, Netherlands: Humanistics University Press, 2004); Mohammad Arkoun, *L'islam morale et politique* [Moral and Political Islam] (Paris: Desclée de Brouwer, 1986); Muhammad Sa'id al-'Ashmawi, *Against Islamic Extremism,* ed. Carolyn Fluehr-Lobban (Gainesville: University Press of Florida, 1998); Ashgar Ali Engineer, *Islam and Liberation Theology: Essays on Liberative Elements in Islam* (New Delhi, India: Sterling, 1990).
15. Sayyid Qutb, *In the Shade of the Qur'an,* Vols. 1–18, trans. M. A. Salahi and A. A. Shamis (Leicester, UK: Islamic Foundation). Not all volumes have been translated.
16. The Arabic romanization used in this book is a simplified version of Library of Congress standards.
17. See Ignatieff, *Human Rights*; Jack Donnelly, *Universal Human Rights in Theory and Practice* (Ithaca, NY: Cornell University Press, 1989).

## CHAPTER 1

1. Hans-Georg Gadamer, *Truth and Method*, trans. Joel Weinsheimer and Donald G. Marshall (New York: Crossroad, 1991), 302.
2. In a Gadamerian framework, a person's religious beliefs exist in fluid relation to other characteristics of identity. One's sense of being also arises out of geography, ethnicity, sex, gender, class, and other forms of personal orientation. Moreover, identity that emerges out of "tradition" need not be limited to religious tradition but might also be associated with other categories of tradition such as ethnic tradition or geographical tradition.
3. Richard Palmer, *Hermeneutics* (Evanston, IL: Northwestern University Press, 1969), 163.
4. Hans-Georg Gadamer, "Reflections on My Philosophical Journey," in *The Philosophy of Hans-Georg Gadamer,* ed. Lewis Edwin Hahn (Peru, IL: Open Court Publishing, 1997), 45. Gadamer notes with hindsight that his emphasis on historical distance in *Truth and Method* should have been expanded to include other types of distance, including cultural distance. Gadamer's notion of "pre-judgments" (*vorurteil*) should not be confused with "prejudices." Prejudgments do not necessarily carry negative connotations; in fact, they are necessary for understanding. They provide structures by which we can perceive the world.
5. Gadamer, *Truth and Method,* 385.
6. Gadamer, *Truth and Method,* 307.
7. Gadamer, *Truth and Method,* 385.
8. Jürgen Habermas, "On Systematically Distorted Communication," *Inquiry* 13, no. 3 (Autumn 1970): 205–18.
9. Susan E. Shapiro, "Rhetoric as Ideology and Critique: The Gadamer-Habermas Debate Reinvented," *Journal of the American Academy of Religion* 62, no. 1 (1994): 128.
10. Habermas, "On Systematically Distorted Communication."
11. Jürgen Habermas, *The Theory of Communicative Action,* vol. 1, *Reason and the Rationalization of Society,* trans. Thomas McCarthy (Boston: Beacon Press, 1984), 332.

12. Thomas McCarthy, *The Critical Theory of Jürgen Habermas* (Cambridge: Polity Press, 1984), 86.
13. Habermas, "On Systematically Distorted Communication," 206.
14. McCarthy, *Critical Theory*, 306.
15. McCarthy, *Critical Theory*, 307.
16. See Jürgen Habermas, " 'Wahrheitstheorien,' Wirklichkeit und Reflexion" in *Festschrift für W. Schulz* [Theories of Truth: Reality and Reflexion in Festschrift for W. Schulz], ed. H. Fahrenbach (Pfüllingen, Germany: Neske, 1973), 211–65.
17. McCarthy, *Critical Theory*, 96–97.
18. McCarthy, *Critical Theory*, 97.
19. See Susan Waltz, "Universal Human Rights: The Contribution of Muslim States," *Human Rights Quarterly* 26, no. 4 (2004): 799–844.
20. Martha Nussbaum, *Women and Human Development: The Capabilities Approach* (Cambridge, MA: University of Cambridge Press, 2000), 167–240; Michael Perry, *The Idea of Human Rights: Four Inquiries* (New York: Oxford University Press, 1998); Amartya Sen, "Human Rights and Asian Values," *Ethics and International Affairs*, ed. Joel Rosenthal (Washington, DC: Georgetown University Press, 1999).
21. Ignatieff, *Human Rights*. Brian Schaefer argues that Ignatieff's approach to human rights is, in fact, not foundationless. See Brian Schaefer, "Human Rights: Problems with the Foundationless Approach," *Social Theory and Practice* 31, no. 1 (January 2005).
22. "Such facts about human beings—that they feel pain, that they can recognize the pain of others, and that they are free to do good and abstain from evil—provide the basis by which we believe that all human beings should be protected from cruelty" (Ignatieff, *Human Rights*, 89). This idea is also the basis of Judith Shklar's work on liberalism in which she examines the universal experience of fear. Liberalism, she claims, should be based on the very basic and human need to live free of fear. Governments that rule by terrorizing the people through random acts of violence, for example, instill both a cruel and an unnecessary fear into the lives of their citizens. Judith Shklar, "The Liberalism of Fear," in *Political Thought and Political Thinkers,* ed. Stanley Hoffman (Chicago: University of Chicago Press, 1998), 3–21.
23. K. Anthony Appiah, in Ignatieff, *Human Rights,* 106.
24. See Ignatieff, *Human Rights,* 87–88, 85, 84.
25. Religions do limit the human ego, particularly when seen from the perspective of theologians such as Reinhold Niebuhr, who see the ego as sinful and gluttonous, but they also affirm the intrinsic worth of human life, which is the message delivered by liberation and feminist theologians.
26. See Abul 'Ala Maududi, *The Islamic Movement: Dynamics of Values, Power, and Change,* ed. Khurram Murad (Leicester, UK: Islamic Foundation, 1984), 101.
27. John Rawls shares with Ignatieff the view of human nature as nonreligious. Although Rawls acknowledges and takes seriously the religious beliefs of citizens, he nonetheless chooses to create a normative conception of the person that he claims is political and moral, rather than religious or philosophical. He describes his conception of the person as "one that begins from our everyday conception of persons as the basic units of thought, deliberation, and responsibility, and adapted to a political conception of justice and not to

a comprehensive doctrine" (Rawls, *Political Liberalism*, 18n20). Although Rawls's normative conception of the person as political reinforces his idea of nonreligious methods of finding consensus, it also moves the discussion further away from the issue of religious difference in pluralistic societies. One of the greatest challenges to liberal societies is that persons descriptively and normatively assert themselves as religious citizens, not simply as political citizens. This complexity, which in many ways supplies Rawls with problems he ultimately hopes to solve, is avoided in the choice to provide a normative anthropology that is politically moral and distinguishable from religiously moral.

28. For example, see Mahnaz Afkhami, ed., *Faith and Freedom: Women's Human Rights in the Muslim World* (Syracuse, NY: Syracuse University Press, 1995); Katie Cannon, *Black Womanist Ethics* (Atlanta: Scholars Press, 1988); Paula Cooey, William R. Eakin, and Jay B. McDaniel, eds., *After Patriarchy: Feminist Transformations of the World Religions* (Maryknoll, NY: Orbis Books, 1993); James Cone, *Black Theology and Black Power* (New York: Seabury Press, 1969); Gustavo Gutierrez, *A Theology of Liberation* (Maryknoll, NY: Orbis Books, 1988); Beverly Harrison, *Making the Connections: Essays in Feminist Social Ethics* (Boston: Beacon Press, 1985).
29. See Mayer, *Islam and Human Rights,* 22. In 1981, delegates from Muslim countries, including Egypt, Pakistan, and Saudi Arabia, under the auspices of the Islamic Council and the Muslim World League, created a parallel document to the UDHR titled the Universal Islamic Declaration of Human Rights. Although it differs from the UDHR in several respects, this document nonetheless represents an effort on behalf of the more conservative elements within Islam to acknowledge both human rights and the traditionalism of their religion. Although Mayer rightly points out the discrepancies between the UDHR and the UIDHR, the acknowledgment of the necessity for human rights marks a necessary step in establishing its universalism.
30. Donnelly argues that the distinctive nature of "rights" should not be conflated with duties to support human dignity. Although I agree with Donnelly that the concept of rights is distinct from that of duties, I disagree with his argument that the concepts of duties and dignity are less valuable than that of "rights" for the progress of human rights globally. See Jack Donnelly, "Human Rights and Human Dignity: An Analytic Critique of Non-Western Conceptions of Human Rights," *American Political Science Review* 76, no. 2 (June 1982): 303–16. See also Amartya Sen, "Elements of a Theory of Human Rights," *Philosophy and Public Affairs* 32, no. 4 (Fall 2004): 318–19, 338–42.
31. Henry Shue, *Basic Rights: Subsistence, Affluence, and U.S. Foreign Policy* (Princeton, NJ: Princeton University Press, 1980).
32. Donnelly, *Universal Human Rights*.
33. Shue, *Basic Rights*, 52–53.
34. Donnelly, *Universal Human Rights,* 50.
35. Donnelly, *Universal Human Rights,* 51.
36. Donnelly, *Universal Human Rights,* 51.
37. Donnelly argues in a similar way regarding African and Chinese traditional cultures. He fails to provide a context in which, for example, African claims to distributive justice or Chinese claims to social obligation can substitute for human rights and correlative duties. A semantic argument against the Chinese reveals little about the actual practices of the culture that may serve

as resources for human rights. To argue that a culture lacks a word that functions as the Western equivalent to "human rights" reveals an emphasis on language over action. Also, other cultures may draw on a vocabulary larger and subtler than the one found in the English language.

38. See, Fazlur Rahman, *Major Themes of the Qur'an* (Minneapolis: Bibliotheca Islamica, 1989), 9.
39. One could also make the argument that on a fundamental level, nonfoundational human rights depend on a belief that the human is simply sacred. Freedom from unnecessary fear, which Ignatieff believes should be the source of human rights, would technically not protect those who do not fear—the mentally incompetent, the very young and perhaps the very old, as well as those who are so abused that normal responses have been suppressed. Ultimately, the prima facie recognition that humans, for whatever reason, should be valued is the impetus for human rights.
40. See Donnelly, "Human Rights and Human Dignity."
41. Nussbaum, *Women and Human Development,* 48–49.
42. Shue opens *Basic Rights* with a quotation from Dom Alano Pena, the Bishop of Marbara, that reveals the importance of this sort of obligation: "Through our work at the community level, we have sought to make the peasant and the worker aware that they have certain basic rights and that they are entitled to exercise those rights. To the military, that is the same thing as subversion." From Larry Rohter, "Brazil's Military, Activist Church Locked in Struggle," *Washington Post*, January 22, 1979, A14.
43. See Charles Beitz, "Human Rights as Common Concern," *American Political Science Review* 95, no. 2 (June 2001): 274.
44. John Rawls, *The Law of Peoples* (Cambridge: Harvard University Press, 1999); Beitz, "Human Rights as Common Concern," 275.
45. Sen, "Elements of a Theory," 320.
46. Beitz, "Human Rights as Common Concern," 273. Beitz believes that fear of paternalism lies behind minimalist approaches to human rights.
47. Note that intervention need not necessarily be militaristic. Intervention can take a number of forms, including observation and monitoring, publication and media reporting, and support of nongovernmental organizations.
48. This example raises the question of whether a majority agreement among nations would constitute a "universal" human right. Although majority rule has never guaranteed the unquestionable morality of a policy, it is arguably the best of our flawed options. Unfortunately, this profound philosophical problem of how humans can come to recognize the perfect form of goodness or justice lies beyond the scope of this book.
49. Ignaz Goldziher, *Introduction to Islamic Theology and Law,* trans. Andras Hamori and Ruth Hamori (Princeton, NJ: Princeton University Press, 1981), 56.
50. Nussbaum, *Women and Human Development.*
51. Nussbaum, *Women and Human Development,* 78–79.
52. Sen, "Elements of a Theory," 330.

## CHAPTER 2

1. In using the term "Islamic" to describe the political thought of Muslim societies, I emphasize the political events and ideas as they relate to the religion of Islam during this time. Islamic political thought might appear redundant, but it is more specific than Muslim political thought, which

would describe the political thought of Muslims, whether or not they relate to Islam.

2. For Americans, this means undertaking the effort to understand not only the colonial events and historical background of Islam but also the way in which Americans are perceived. Although in the first half of the twentieth century, the United States played an indirect role in the colonialism of Muslim countries, it has since become identified with the major colonizing countries of that time. American imperialism asserts massive military and economic power over other countries. See, Ania Loomba, *Colonialism/ Postcolonialism* (New York: Routledge, 1998), 6–7.
3. Anouar Majid offers a critique of the limits of postcolonial theory, particularly with regard to the diversity within Islam, in his *Unveiling Traditions: Postcolonial Islam in a Polycentric World* (Durham: Duke University Press, 2000). See also Homi Bhabha, *The Location of Culture* (New York: Routledge, 1994); Frantz Fanon, *A Dying Colonialism* (New York: Grove Press, 1965); Timothy Mitchell, *Colonizing Egypt* (Berkeley and Los Angeles: University of California Press, 1991); and Edward Said, *Culture and Imperialism* (New York: Knopf, 1993).
4. The notable exception of witness as individual practice is consistent with the idea, to be discussed later, of freedom of conscience. The oft-quoted Qur'anic injunction that "there shall be no compulsion in religion" (2:256) suggests that a person witnesses God as a matter of individual conscience and should not be coerced by the state or another person.
5. All dates are in the Common Era.
6. Hamid Enayat, *Modern Islamic Political Thought* (Austin: University of Texas Press, 1982), 6.
7. Marshall G. S. Hodgson, *The Venture of Islam*, vol. 1, *The Classical Age of Islam* (Chicago: University of Chicago Press, 1975), 83.
8. The differences between the Sunni and Shi'i, although temporarily ameliorated in the twentieth century when they were united against the colonizing West, were at times so extreme that they considered each other more heretical than even Jews or Christians. Prior to the sixteenth century and the rise of the Safavid and Ottoman rules, Sunni and Shi'i leaders were relatively tolerant of persons belonging to the other school. Differences arose markedly, however, with the installation of Shah Isma'il, the founder of the Safavid dynasty (1501–1736), which established Shi'ism as the official religion. His first act as shah was to institute the public cursing of the first three caliphs, who were revered by Sunnis and Ottomans. In the early sixteenth century, Sultan Selim I exterminated thousands of Shi'i Muslims, an act returned with the suppression of Sunnism by the Safavids. The doctrinal differences between the Sunnis and Shi'ites, together with desire to control each other's territories, fueled a series of wars between the two dynasties. See Nikki Keddie, "Is There a Middle East?" *International Journal of Middle East Studies* 4, no. 3 (July 1973): 259.
9. Enayat, *Modern Islamic Political Thought,* 6.
10. Enayat, *Modern Islamic Political Thought,* 30.
11. Marshall Hodgson, *The Venture of Islam,* vol. 3, *The Gunpowder Empires and Modern Times* (Chicago: University of Chicago Press, 1977), 192, 225.
12. Fanon in *The Wretched of the Earth* argues that the violence used by the Algerian resistance movement is a fair imitation of the violence first used by

the French colonizers against them. See Frantz Fanon, *The Wretched of the Earth,* trans. Constance Farrington (New York: Grove Press), 1963, 88–95.

13. Hodgson, *Venture of Islam,* 3:229.
14. Hodgson, *Venture of Islam,* 3:233.
15. Bhabha discusses in detail the ostensibly innocuous learning of English, French, Dutch, and other European languages. He uses the term "mimicry" to describe the strategy used by colonizers to create an Other who is ambiguously both like them and unlike them. It involves the imitation of speech and mannerisms and the adoption of similar values by the colonized to facilitate the process of colonization. Mimicry also enables the colonizers to distinguish between "good natives," those who mimic, and "bad natives," those who do not, and therefore to divide the native population. The primary distinguishing feature between the colonizer and the mimic is race. Occasionally, colonized persons will "mimic" to such an extent that they surpass the standards of cultural excellence set by the colonizers. The fact that the colonized person is usually nonwhite, however, sets up a permanent barrier between the colonizer and the colonized. Bhabha is indebted to Fanon's work in *Black Skins, White Masks,* which lays the groundwork for Bhabha's analysis of mimicry. See Homi Bhabha, "Of Mimicry and Man: The Ambivalence of Colonial Discourse," *October* 28 (1984): 125–33; Frantz Fanon, *Black Skins, White Masks* (New York: Grove Press, 1968). Wole Soyinka offers a dramatic interpretation of mimicry in *Death and the King's Horseman,* a tragedy that centers on the ritual suicide of a village leader, his seemingly "Europeanized" son, and British colonizers in Africa. Wole Soyinka, *Death and the King's Horseman* (New York: Hill and Wang, 1975).
16. Marxist theory readily applies to the phenomenon of class division through the expansion of colonialism. Postcolonial theorists draw heavily on Marx's writings and Lenin's *Imperialism, the Highest Stage of Capitalism* in their analyses of modern colonialism. Louis Althusser's reformulation of Marxist theory, which emphasizes the power of ideology over economics, has been particularly influential in determining the influence of institutions to perpetuate class difference. The theories of Marxist philosopher Antonio Gramsci concerning the possibility of struggle against hegemonies has also been seminal in postcolonial studies. See Louis Althusser, "Ideological State Apparatuses," in *Lenin and Philosophy* (London: New Left Books, 1971), 127–86; Aimè Cèsaire, *Discourse on Colonialism,* trans. Joan Pinkham (New York: Monthly Review Press, 2000); Antonio Gramsci, *A Gramsci Reader: Selected Writings, 1916–1935* (London: Lawrence and Wishart, 2000); Fanon, *Wretched of the Earth.*
17. Loomba explains the particularly invasive nature of colonial economies: "Modern colonialism did more than extract tribute, goods and wealth from the countries that it conquered—it restructured the economies of the latter, drawing them into a complex relationship with their own, so that there was a flow of human and natural resources between the colonized and colonial countries. This flow worked in both directions—slaves and indentured labour as well as raw materials were transported to manufacture goods in the metropolis, or in other locations for metropolitan consumption, but the colonies also provided captive markets for European goods. . . . In whichever direction human beings and materials traveled, the profits always flowed back into the so-called 'mother country'" (Loomba, *Colonialism,* 3–4).

18. Richard King and Jyotsna Singh apply postcolonial theory to Indian culture. See Richard King, *Orientalism and Religion: Postcolonial Theory, India, and the "Mystic East"* (New York: Routledge, 1999); Jyotsna Singh, *Colonial Narratives/Cultural Dialogues: "Discoveries" of India in the Language of Colonialism* (New York: Routledge, 1996).
19. See Enayat, *Modern Islamic Political Thought*, 101–10, for a summary of Maududi's political thought.
20. See Sayyed Nasr, *The Vanguard of the Islamic Revolution: The Jama'at-i Islami of Pakistan* (Berkeley and Los Angeles: University of California Press, 1994) for a historical treatment of the Jama'at-i Islami and an analysis of the political and historical events that form the context of its establishment.
21. When Fatimah Jinnah ran for president of Pakistan in 1965, Maududi supported her candidacy, much to the outrage of the traditionalist religious establishment. See Enayat, *Modern Islamic Political Thought,* 110.
22. For a detailed yet accessible overview of the political and military history of Egypt during this period, see Al-Sayyid Marsot, *A Short History of Modern Egypt* (New York: Cambridge University Press, 1985), 54–131. For a more general history of Egypt during the first half of the twentieth century, see William Cleveland, *A History of the Modern Middle East,* 3rd ed. (Boulder, CO: Westview Press, 2004), 193–208.
23. Ibrahim Abu Rabi', *Intellectual Origins of Islamic Resurgence in the Modern Arab World* (Albany: State University of New York Press, 1996), 93.
24. Keddie believes that Ottoman Turkey and Egypt similarly benefited from a history of government centralization. See Keddie, "Middle East," 266.
25. The Mut'azila school refers to an eighth-century theological movement that harmonized human rationality and revelation. It opposed the Ash'ari school, which held that morality was determined by divine command alone. On the relevance of the theological thought of 'Abduh and Ghazali to politics and society, see Malcolm Kerr, *Islamic Reform: The Political and Legal Theories of Muhammad Abduh and Rashid Rida* (Berkeley and Los Angeles: University of California Press, 1966), and Sherman Jackson, *On the Boundaries of Theological Tolerance in Islam: Abu Hamid al-Ghazali's Faysal al-Tafriqa* (New York: Oxford University Press, 2002).
26. Keddie explores Afghani's religious response to colonialism in Nikki Keddie, *An Islamic Response to Imperialism: Political and Religious Writings of Sayyid Jamal al-Din al-Afghani* (Berkeley and Los Angeles: University of California Press, 1983).
27. Hans Wehr, *A Dictionary of Modern Written Arabic,* 3rd ed., ed. J. Milton Cowan (Beirut: Librairie du Liban, 1980), 786.
28. Wael Hallaq, *A History of Islamic Legal Theories: An Introduction to Sunni usul al-fiqh* (New York: Cambridge University Press, 1997), 212.
29. See Kerr, *Islamic Reform.*
30. Albert Hourani, *A History of the Arab Peoples* (Cambridge, MA: Belknap Press of Harvard University Press), 258, 308. Particularly when faced with a colonizing presence that proudly identifies itself as "rationalist" and "modern," the resistance movement among the colonized is left in a quandary. Does it also identify itself as rationalist and modern, thereby imitating its colonizers, or does it turn to traditionalism and against representations of modernity? The colonizers have frustratingly defined the options for the colonized, even in resistance, by creating a trenchant dichotomy between the colonizers and the

colonized. Said points out a number of these oppositions that come out of European self-conception: rational/irrational, civilized/barbaric, masculine/feminine, diligent/lazy, oversexed/controlled. With regard to the theological response to colonialism, the options for self-identity left to the colonized in resistance are invariably tainted. See Edward Said, *Orientalism* (New York: Vintage, 1978), 45–49; Loomba, *Colonialism,* 47.

31. Keddie asserts that historically "change was forced upon the Ottomans and not upon the Persians. . . . Iran, unlike the core areas of the Ottoman Empire and Egypt, was a vast, sparely populated area with high mountains and large deserts, where the central government had to share its power with a mixed group of ruling classes comprising tribal leaders, ulama, large landlords, and even partially independent governors and other governmental officials. Particularly during the nineteenth century there was much less integration and centralization of the country and its ruling class than in the Ottoman Empire and Egypt, as neither the ulama nor the tribes was brought to heel and no significant centralized army or bureaucracy was built" (Keddie, "Middle East," 261, 266). Colonizers would prove both incapable of and unwilling to put in the immense effort required to bring historically decentralized Iran under imperial control.
32. Elton Daniel, *The History of Iran* (Westport, CT: Greenwood Press, 2000), 115–17.
33. For a detailed history of the creation of Iran as a modern nation-state, see Daniel, *History of Iran,* 115–41.
34. Although Reza Shah differed from Kemal, he was nonetheless influenced and inspired by the success of his reforms. Ideas borrowed from Kemal included state-financed factories, the unveiling and limited emancipation of women, and secular education. Reza Shah even wanted to establish an Iranian republic, but was dissuaded by the ulama, who successfully argued for a more traditional dynasty instead. See Keddie, "Middle East," 268.
35. For a full account of Soroush's intellectual influences and development, see 'Abdolkarim Soroush, "Intellectual Autobiography: An Interview," in *Reason, Freedom, and Democracy in Islam: Essential Writings of 'Abdolkarim Soroush* (New York: Oxford University Press, 2000), 3–25.
36. For details concerning the long reign of Reza Shah, see, Daniel, *History of Iran,* 144–73.

## CHAPTER 3

1. For theoretical and comparative studies on democracy, see Robert Dahl, *On Democracy* (New Haven, CT: Yale University Press, 1998); David Held, *Models of Democracy* (Stanford, CA: Stanford University Press, 1996); Arend Lijphart, *Patterns of Democracy: Government Forms and Performance in Thirty-Six Countries* (New Haven, CT: Yale University Press, 1999); Amartya Sen, "Democracy as a Universal Value," *Journal of Democracy* 10, no. 3 (1999): 3–17.
2. Khaled Abou El Fadl, "Islam and the Challenge of Democracy," *Boston Review,* April/May 2003. El Fadl argues that Islam and democracy are inherently compatible and share many of the same values. El Fadl shares this view with several other scholars. See John Esposito and John Voll, *Islam and Democracy* (New York: Oxford University Press, 1996); Abdulaziz Sachedina, *The Islamic Roots of Democratic Pluralism* (New York:

Oxford University Press, 2001); Azzam Tamimi, *Rachid Ghannouchi: A Democrat within Islamism* (New York: Oxford University Press, 2000).

3. Abul A'la Maududi, *Human Rights in Islam* (Lahore, Pakistan: Islamic Publications, 1977), 7. Maududi is concerned to present an unabashedly positive, at times overly simplistic view of Islam. He offers, for example, the following apologetic descriptions of Islam: The "history of the Muslims, apart from a few lapses of the individuals here or there, has been free from this crime [of rape in war] against womanhood." "Islam tried to solve the problem of the slaves that were in Arabia by encouraging people in different ways to set their slaves free. . . . The result of this policy was that by the time the period of the Rightly-Guided Caliphs was reached, all the old slaves of Arabia were liberated." "The rules which have been framed by Islam to make war civilized and humane, are in the nature of law, because they are the injunctions of God and His Prophet which are followed by Muslims in all circumstances, regardless of the behaviour of the enemy" (Maududi, *Human Rights*, 16, 18, 35). Maududi appears to engage in the re-creation of local culture that has been destroyed as a result of colonialism. Because "it is part of imperialist strategy to destroy indigenous culture, and a major aspect of that is to refuse to allow it a past of any worth, the recovery and revaluing of history and culture has a considerable part to play in resistance movements" (Peter Childs and R. J. Patrick Williams, *An Introduction to Post-Colonial Theory* [New York: Prentice Hall, 1997], 55). Maududi's efforts to resist the lingering influence of colonialism include this apologetic history. Fanon, trained in psychology, notes the beneficial psychological effect on colonized people of critiquing oppressive ideologies and rewriting histories that deny the injustice of colonialism. See Fanon, *Dying Colonialism.*
4. In an earlier work Maududi describes Islamic democracy as "theo-democracy," which is "a divine democratic government." Under a theo-democracy, "Muslims have been given a limited popular sovereignty under the suzerainty of God. The executive under this system of government is constituted by the general will of the Muslims who also have the right to depose it. All administrative matters and all questions about which no explicit injunction is to be found in this *shari'ah* are settled by the consensus of opinion among the Muslims. . . . But . . . it is a theocracy in the sense that where an explicit command of God of His Prophet already exists, no Muslim leader or legislature, or any religious scholar can form an independent judgment, not even all the Muslims of the world put together, have any right to make the least alteration in it" (*The Islamic Law and Constitution,* trans. Khurshid Ahmad [Lahore, Pakistan: Islamic Publications, 1960], 148).
5. Maududi, *Human Rights*, 6. *Khilafa* refers to the representation of God's will on earth by humankind.
6. Maududi, *Human Rights*, 7; Maududi, *Islamic Movement,* 96.
7. Maududi, *Islamic Movement,* 101–2.
8. Maududi, *Islamic Movement,* 101.
9. Maududi, *Islamic Movement,* 79, 72, 73. Maududi at times appears to send conflicting messages about non-Muslims. Although he often speaks of "moral" people without specifying religious affiliation, at other times he refers specifically to *ahl al-kitab* (the People of the Book, i.e., Jews and Christians) and oftentimes refers to Muslims alone. Maududi intimates that a hierarchy exists: at the bottom are immoral people, followed by moral pagans, followed by Jews and Christians, and then Muslims at the top. He explains that "those

individuals who in the *Jahiliyyah* [literally ignorance, referring to the period before the advent of Islam] showed great ability and firmness of character, would continue in their Islamic phase to be dynamic and creative. But there would be a key difference: formerly their abilities were directed along the wrong lines, while after their acceptance of Islam, they would begin to follow the right course" (Maududi, *Islamic Movement,* 96).

10. Maududi, *Islamic Movement,* 71.
11. Sayyid Qutb, *Social Justice in Islam,* trans. John B. Hardie (New York: Octagon Books, 1970), 88, 31, 8, 69. (In Arabic, Sayyid Qutb, *Al-'Adalah al-ijtima' iyah fi al-Islam* [Beirut: Eastern House, 1975]).
12. Qutb, *Social Justice*, 31.
13. Qutb, *Social Justice*, 30. Qutb uses these phrases in the original Arabic: *al-tahrir al-wijdani* (freedom of conscience), *al-musawah al-insaniyya* (human equality), and *al-takaful al-ijtima'i* (mutual responsibility in society).
14. Qutb, *Social Justice*, 43.
15. Qutb writes about gender discrimination as well (*Social Justice,* 49–53). With regard to differences in equality between men and women, Qutb asserts that Islam advocates the spiritual and material equality of men and women. The difference in proportions of inheritance between sons and daughters, whereby sons are entitled to more than daughters, Qutb explains as necessary given social and cultural expectations of marriage. Women are allowed to keep what they bring into a marriage. Because men are expected to provide for their wives and children, as well as for their parents in old age, however, sons receive more of their parents' wealth than women. Differences in inheritance are not intended to leave women poor and men wealthy. Qutb also points out that Islam encourages women to learn and to gain an education. Education not only serves practical purposes in women's everyday lives but also contributes to their spiritual advancement.

    Qutb, like Maududi, compares Islamic and Western standards of equality for women. With regard to the possession of property by women in Islam, he compares the situation of women in Islamic countries to those in France. At the time (in the 1940s), women in France could make decisions concerning their property only through a male guardian. Women in Islam, on the other hand, have always maintained the right to administer their property without the consent of a man. He also observes that although women in France are not legally permitted to manage their own assets, they are legally allowed "the right of every kind of unchastity, public or private" (*Social Justice,* 53), a right that Islam forbids for both men and women. Qutb argues that women who work in the United States and Europe are employed merely to the advantage of men and their businesses. He points to the women who work in "slavery and servitude" (*Social Justice,* 53) because they are both paid less than men and often hired to use their attractiveness in order to glean information from men or to extract profit from them. Women in the West need to work, he claims, because their husbands have shirked their duties as providers. Women have no choice but to exploit themselves in degrading ways. He extrapolates that due to the inequality in wages between the sexes, women in the West sought suffrage in order to correct this injustice, and then they sought representation in government in order to ensure equality. Qutb both condemns the situation of women in the West and sees their increasingly public roles through a sympathetic lens.

16. Compare to John Rawls's principle of equality of opportunity. The principles of justice that Rawls offers as guidelines for how basic institutions may realize the values of liberty and equality are as follows: "a) Each person has an equal claim to a fully adequate scheme of equal basic rights and liberties, which scheme is compatible with the same scheme for all; and in this scheme the equal political liberties, and only those liberties, are to be guaranteed their fair value; b) Social and economic inequalities are to satisfy two conditions: first they are to be attached to positions and offices open to all under conditions of fair equality of opportunity; and second, they are to be to the greatest benefit of the least advantaged members of society" (Rawls, *Political Liberalism,* 5–6).
17. Qutb, *Social Justice,* 28.
18. Qutb, *Social Justice,* 110.
19. Qutb, *Social Justice,* 98, 110.
20. Qutb, *Social Justice,* 44.
21. Qutb, *Social Justice,* 32.
22. Qutb, *Social Justice,* 95, 96.
23. Qutb, *Social Justice,* 93, 97.
24. Qutb, *Social Justice,* 97. Religious duties taken from the Arabic *al-fara'id.*
25. See Shklar, "Liberalism of Fear." Once governments agree that such lines dividing the public from the private should be drawn, they can begin to negotiate where those lines should be drawn. From Shklar's perspective, human rights violations occur when governments fail to draw any distinction between public and private.
26. Qutb, *Social Justice,* 97–98.
27. Qutb, *Social Justice,* 95, 96.
28. Soroush, "Tolerance and Governance: A Discourse on Religion and Democracy," in *Reason, Freedom, and Democracy*, 134, 122; Soroush, "The Idea of a Democratic Religious Government," in *Reason, Freedom, and Democracy,* 126.
29. Soroush, "Idea of a Democratic Religious Government," 126.
30. Soroush, "Idea of a Democratic Religious Government," 126.
31. Whether democracy precedes or follows economic development remains a highly debated issue. Many human rights thinkers fear that the arguments for economic development as prior to democracy leave the door open for oppressive political regimes, which claim that human rights must be suspended in the short term in order to obtain rapid economic development. See Donnelly, *Universal Human Rights,* 161–202.
32. Soroush, "Life and Virtue: The Relationship between Socioeconomic Development and Ethics," in *Reason, Freedom, and Democracy,* 45.
33. Soroush, "Life and Virtue," 45.
34. Soroush, "Life and Virtue," 46.
35. Soroush, "Life and Virtue," 46.
36. Soroush, "Life and Virtue," 46.
37. Here arises the question of whether scientific advancement precedes human rights (in this case, a democratic government) or whether a democratic government enables people to advance scientific knowledge. Although empirical evidence indicates that scientific advances certainly occur in nondemocratic societies, such as the former Soviet Union and Communist China, democratic societies appear to apply and disseminate these advances more rapidly, particularly in the form of technology.

38. Soroush, "Life and Virtue," 46.
39. Soroush, "Idea of a Democratic Religious Government," 127; Soroush, "Tolerance and Governance," 131.
40. Soroush, "Tolerance and Governance," 144. See also Valla Vakili, "Abdolkarim Soroush and Critical Discourse in Iran," in John Esposito and John Voll, eds., *Makers of Contemporary Islam* (New York: Oxford University Press, 2001), 155.
41. Fazlur Rahman argues similarly that there is a distinction between the law and the Law of Islam. *Shari'a*, Islamic jurisprudence, can only hope to approximate the true Law of Islam. Jurisprudence should not be mistaken for the faith itself. See Fazlur Rahman, "Law and Ethics in Islam," in *Ethics in Islam: Ninth Giorgio Levi Della Vida Biennial Conference,* ed. Richard G. Hovannisian (Malibu, CA: Undeila Publications, 1985).
42. Soroush, "Tolerance and Governance," 143.
43. Soroush, "Idea of a Democratic Religious Government," 128.
44. Qutb, *Social Justice*, 43, 72; Soroush, "Life and Virtue," 45.
45. Maududi, *Human Rights*, 7; Qutb, *Social Justice,* 31; Soroush, "Idea of a Democratic Religious Government," 127.
46. Qutb, *Social Justice,* 44; Soroush, "Life and Virtue," 45.
47. Qutb, *Social Justice,* 30, 43.
48. Soroush, "Life and Virtue," 45–46.
49. Sen, "Human Rights and Asian Values," 173.
50. Heiner Bielefeldt, "Muslim Voices in the Human Rights Debate," *Human Rights Quarterly* 17, no. 4 (1995): 587–617.
51. Qutb, *Social Justice*, 30; Soroush, "Tolerance and Governance," 147–48.
52. Soroush, "Intellectual Autobiography," in *Reason, Freedom, and Democracy,* 21.
53. The writings of the three thinkers, despite their postcolonial circumstances, appear to welcome the free exchange of ideas with European theorists. Qutb's sympathetic ear for Marxist theory, for example, is shared with Fanon and Cèsaire. Moreover, the Marxist philosophy of Althusser is helpful in understanding Qutb's own understanding of the role of such institutions as schools and the media as "State Apparatuses," which enable the perpetuation of colonialism through ideology. Whereas some colonial institutions, such as the army or police, are blunt instruments of colonial power, such seemingly benign institutions as schools and hospitals are important for creating consent to colonialism among the colonized. In "modern capitalist societies, [force] is achieved by 'Repressive State Apparatuses' such as the army and the police, but the latter is enforced via 'Ideological State Apparatuses' such as schools, the Church, the family, media, and political systems. . . . Such an idea is immensely useful in demystifying certain apparently innocent and apolitical institutions and has subsequently influenced analyses of schools, universities, family structures, and (via the work of Althusser's friend Pierre Macherey) literary texts" (Loomba, *Colonialism,* 33).
54. Qutb, *Social Justice,* 44, 98, 31.
55. Qutb, *Social Justice,* 95.
56. Maududi, *Islamic Movement,* 71, 72.
57. Soroush, "Tolerance and Governance," 143.
58. Soroush, "Idea of a Democratic Religious Government," 127.
59. Soroush, "Islamic Revival and Reform: Theological Approaches," in *Reason, Freedom, and Democracy,* 31.

60. See Abdolkarim Soroush, "The Evolution and Devolution of Religious Knowledge," in *Liberal Islam: A Sourcebook,* ed. Charles Kurzman, 244–51 (New York: Oxford University Press, 1998). Kurzman groups Soroush with other prominent Islamic thinkers who advocate freedom of thought in Islam. Soroush's peers include 'Ali Shari'ati (Iran, 1933–1977), Yusuf Al-Qaradawi (Egypt-Qatar, b. 1926), Mohamed Arkoun (Algeria-France, b. 1928), Abdullahi Ahmed An-Na'im (Sudan-United States, b. 1946), and Alhaji Adeleke Dirisu Ajijola (Nigeria, b. 1932).
61. For additional information about these fundamentalist characteristics, see Mark Juergensmeyer, *Terror in the Mind of God: The Global Rise of Religious Violence* (Berkeley and Los Angeles: University of California Press, 2000) and Bruce Lawrence, *Defenders of God: The Fundamentalist Revolt against the Modern Age* (Columbia: University of South Carolina Press, 1989).
62. See Keddie, "Middle East." The shared past of Sunni and Shi'ite Muslims extends only until the death of Muhammad. The struggle for Muhammad's succession, bitter wars between Sunni and Shi'ite dynasties, and the regular suppression of Sunnis within Shi'ite territory and Shi'ites within Sunni territory taint the possibility for a shared glorious past. Keddie points out that whereas the four Caliphs are revered in Sunni culture, pre-Islamic heroes are celebrated in Shi'ite culture. This may be due to the small numbers of Shi'ites relative to Sunnis. The adulation of pre-Islamic heroes in Persia, for example, enabled collective support across territories where several religious traditions, including Shi'ism, might be found. Nevertheless, in the face of a Western common enemy, such divisions have been put aside.
63. Qutb, *Social Justice*, 49–53, 94.
64. Maududi, *Islamic Movement,* 96; Maududi, *Human Rights,* 7.
65. Soroush, "Doctrine and Justification," in *Reason, Freedom, and Democracy,* 72.
66. For an examination of various ethical traditions within Islam, see Majid Fakhry, *Ethical Theories in Islam* (Leiden, Netherlands: E. J. Brill, 1991), and George Hourani, *Reason and Tradition in Islamic Ethics* (Cambridge: Cambridge University Press, 1985).
67. Soroush, "The Sense and Essence of Secularism," in *Reason, Freedom and Democracy,* 65–66. Soroush does not conclude that the Mu'tazilites were able to combine Greek philosophy and religion successfully, but leaves open the possibility that philosophy generally and religion are entirely compatible. For philosophical background to Mu'tazilite ethics, see Fakhry, *Ethical Theories,* 31–45.
68. Fakhry, *Ethical Theories,* 46–58.

## CHAPTER 4

1. In the case of Christianity, Christopher Marshall presents a study tracing the links between biblical themes and concepts found in the Universal Declaration of Human Rights. See Christopher Marshall, *Crowned with Glory and Honor: Human Rights in the Biblical Tradition* (Scottsdale, PA: Herald Press, 2002). With regard to Islamic thought, Fazlur Rahman defines *taqwa* as "that inner torch . . . where by [one] can discern between right and wrong. . . . He is to use the torch primarily against his own self-deception in assessing and judging his actions" (Rahman, *Major Themes,* 9). Associated with

*taqwa* is the term *hidaya*, "guidance," which is "kneaded into man's primordial nature insofar as the distinction between good and evil is 'ingrained in his heart' (91:8)" (Rahman, *Major Themes,* 9). (Compare to Romans 2:14–15 [New Revised Standard Version], "When Gentiles, who do not possess the law, do instinctively what the law requires, these, though not having the law, are a law to themselves. They show that what the law requires is written on their hearts, to which their own conscience also bears witness.")

2. Toleration, of course, is not limited to internal characteristics, such as religious belief. Toleration applies as well to generally more external and readily observable characteristics such as race, ethnicity, and sex.
3. Maududi, *Human Rights,* 29–30.
4. Maududi, "Islamic Political Framework," *Human Rights,* 9; see also Maududi, *Islamic Law,* 129–61. Maududi offers consistent arguments on this point. In his essay titled "Fallacy of Rationalism," he states, "If one speaks as a non-Muslim, he will have every right to criticize the principles and injunctions enunciated by the Quran in whatever manner he likes, because he does not believe in the holy Quran as the final word of Allah. But, speaking as a non-Muslim, he will have no right to pose himself as a Muslim and try to explain to the Muslims the meanings of Islam and the ways and means to promote Islam" (*West versus Islam,* trans. S. Waqar Ahmad Gardezi and Abdul Waheed Khan [New Delhi, India: International Islamic Publishers, 1992], in Mansoor Moaddel and Kamran Talattof, eds., *Contemporary Debates in Islam: An Anthology of Modernist and Fundamentalist Thought* [New York: St. Martin's Press, 2000], 210).
5. Maududi, *Human Rights,* 24.
6. Maududi, *Human Rights,* 24.
7. Maududi, *Human Rights,* 30.
8. In the founding years of Islam, "idol worship" was especially prevalent on the Arabian Peninsula. The region served as a nexus for traders from the east and west, which meant that travelers of various religious traditions worked and rested there. The peaceful coexistence of multiple religious faiths was necessary if the region was to survive as a trading center.
9. Maududi, "Islamic Political Framework," 9. See also Maududi, *Islamic Law,* 129–61.
10. Maududi, *Human Rights,* 28.
11. This is certainly the case for Islamic states. Maududi suggests that even non-Islamic states that include Muslims among its citizens would be violating their own laws about respecting freedom of conscience if they were to prohibit Muslims from enjoining the good and forbidding evil.
12. Maududi, *Human Rights,* 28.
13. Maududi states his argument as follows: if a religious group attempts to "foist its ideology on others by violent means and endangers the security of the State or its administration, necessary action shall certainly be taken against it" (*Islamic Law,* 268). He does not clarify what "necessary action" entails, but the position that he articulates about limiting religious belief that entails violence seems reasonable. There are, of course, controversial exceptions to this general statement about religious belief and violence, but Maududi does not here discuss them.
14. Maududi, *Human Rights,* 28.
15. Maududi, *Human Rights,* 29, 30.
16. Maududi, *Human Rights,* 28.

17. Maududi, *Human Rights,* 28.
18. Qutb, *Social Justice,* 44.
19. See Jon Elster, *An Introduction to Karl Marx* (New York: Cambridge University Press, 1990), 168–85. "When we refer to a view as an instance of *false* consciousness—a frequently used term for ideological thinking—we do not simply label it as an error or misperception, a thought that is false to the facts. We suggest that it is falsified and distorted in a systematic way, by causal processes that impede the search for truth. Unlike an accidental mistake, which offers little resistance to correction . . . ideologies are shaped by deep-seated tendencies that help them survive criticism and refutation for a long time" (Elster, *Marx,* 168).
20. Qutb, *Social Justice,* 31, 44, 32.
21. Qutb, *Social Justice,* 32.
22. Qutb, *Social Justice,* 32, 33.
23. Sayyid Qutb, "Islam as the Foundation of Knowledge," in Moaddel and Talattof, *Contemporary Debates,* 201. As previously noted, Qutb's strategy against imperialism reinforces postcolonial theories describing the power of ideology in maintaining dominance. Although military force and political force are obvious methods used by colonial powers to suppress the local population, other institutions are also necessary for maintaining control. Schools and hospitals ostensibly seem to be innocent institutions, but they are important for legitimizing colonial presence. Moreover, the lessons taught at schools, which require the use of European texts and literature and demand facility in a nonnative tongue, help to reinforce the permanence of the occupation. These nonmilitary institutions impress on the locals the supposed superiority of the colonizing culture over the native one. Qutb attempts to remove these lingering colonial trappings through a purging of humanistic and social scientific texts and by reinforcing Islam as a more indigenous source of knowledge that is, it is hoped, untainted by Europeans. See Jacques Derrida, *Writing and Difference* (Chicago: University of Chicago Press, 1980); Michel Foucault, *The History of Sexuality: An Introduction* (New York: Vintage, 1990); Pierre Macherey, *A Theory of Literary Production* (Boston: Routledge and Kegan Paul, 1978); Ferdinand Saussure, *Course in General Linguistics* (Chicago: Open Court Publishing, 1988). See also Loomba, *Colonialism,* 36–37.
24. Qutb, *Social Justice,* 36, 45.
25. Qutb, *Social Justice,* 45.
26. Soroush, "Tolerance and Governance," in *Reason, Freedom, and Democracy,* 144; Rahman, "Law and Ethics."
27. Soroush, "Tolerance and Governance," 135.
28. Soroush, "Tolerance and Governance," 142, 143.
29. Soroush, "Tolerance and Governance," 144.
30. Soroush, "Reason and Freedom," in *Reason, Freedom, and Democracy,* 103.
31. Soroush, "Reason and Freedom," 103.
32. Soroush, "Reason and Freedom," 97; Soroush, "Idea of a Democratic Religious Government," in *Reason, Freedom, and Democracy*, 128.
33. Soroush, "Reason and Freedom," 90–91.
34. Soroush, "Reason and Freedom," 90–91.
35. Soroush, "Reason and Freedom," 91.
36. Soroush, "Reason and Freedom," 98. The *Mathnavi* refers to the thirteenth-century Sufi mystic Rumi's seven volumes of poetry.

37. Soroush, "Reason and Freedom," 100. Note here how Soroush uses *jihad* to mean not physical force but rather a metaphorical "war" against lies. *Jihad* in this sense might mean to use the press to present fair, objective, and accurate information, to educate people on topics that they may not understand clearly, and to engage in debates and conversations so that more than one side of an issue may be voiced. See also "Reason and Freedom," 99.
38. Soroush, "Reason and Freedom," 104.
39. Soroush, "Reason and Freedom," 91.
40. Soroush, "Tolerance and Governance," 145.
41. Soroush, "Intellectual Autobiography," in *Reason, Freedom, and Democracy,* 22.
42. Soroush, "Tolerance and Governance," 135, 144.
43. Maududi, *Human Rights*, 7, 30; Sayyid Qutb, "Jihad in the Cause of Allah," in Moaddel and Talattof, *Contemporary Debates,* 225; Qutb, *Social Justice,* 12, 93–94.
44. Maududi, *Human Rights,* 24, 28.
45. Maududi, *Human Rights,* 28; Qutb, "Islam as the Foundation," 201; Qutb, *Social Justice,* 49–53.
46. Soroush, "Reason and Freedom," 104.
47. Maududi, *Human Rights,* 24, 28.
48. Maududi, *Human Rights,* 28–30.
49. Qutb, *Social Justice,* 31.
50. Qutb, *Social Justice,* 44.
51. Qutb, "Islam as the Foundation," 201.
52. Soroush, "Reason and Freedom," 104.
53. Soroush, "Reason and Freedom," 97.
54. Soroush, "Tolerance and Governance," 142.
55. Fakhry, *Ethical Theories,* 31–58.
56. Keddie, "Middle East," 262–66.
57. For a range of liberal Islamic thought, see al-ʻAshmawy, *Against Islamic Extremism*; An-Naʻim, *Toward an Islamic Reformation;* Khaled Abou El Fadl, *The Place of Tolerance in Islam,* ed. Joshua Cohen and Ian Lague (Boston: Beacon Press, 2002); Esposito and Voll, *Makers of Contemporary Islam;* Kurzman, *Liberal Islam;* Fatima Mernissi, The *Veil and the Male Elite: A Feminist Interpretation of Women's Rights in Islam,* trans. Mary Jo Lakeland (Reading, MA: Addison-Wesley, 1991); Fazlur Rahman, *Islam and Modernity* (Chicago: University of Chicago Press, 1982); Sachedina, *Islamic Roots;* Omid Safi, ed., *Progressive Muslims: On Justice, Gender, and Pluralism* (Oxford: Oneworld, 2003); Amina Wadud, *Qur'an and Woman: Rereading the Sacred Text from a Woman's Perspective* (New York: Oxford University Press, 1999).

## CHAPTER 5

1. Michael Walzer, *On Toleration* (New Haven, CT: Yale University Press, 1997), xi.
2. Maududi, *Human Rights*, 8, 9. Although he does not state gender or sex in the statement about discrimination, Maududi in fact supported a woman candidate, Fatima Jinnah, for the office of president of Pakistan in 1965. He stated that although a woman as president was not ideal, it was possible. See Enayat, *Modern Islamic Political Thought*, 110.

3. Maududi, *Islamic Law*, 149; Maududi, *Human Rights,* 30.
4. Abul A'la Maududi, *Let Us Be Muslims,* ed. Khurram Murad (Leicester, UK: Islamic Foundation, 1985), 100.
5. Compare this to major disagreements within the Christian tradition concerning the Trinity of God, the divinity of Jesus Christ, or the characterization of the papacy.
6. Maududi, *Let Us Be Muslims,* 130, 132.
7. Maududi, *Let Us Be Muslims,* 132; Maududi, "Fallacy," in Moaddel and Talattof, *Contemporary Debates,* 213, 210.
8. Maududi and Qutb share similar understandings of the insidious nature of colonialist discourse, which enables the perpetuation of an ideology of compliance among the colonized. Although he does not state explicitly, as Qutb does, the specific humanistic and social scientific disciplines that are more culpable than the hard sciences, Maududi mentions schools and the teaching of English as ways in which colonialist ideology is transmitted. His fear of the indoctrination of colonialist culture and values finds voice in Bhabha's concept of mimicry.
9. Maududi, "Fallacy," 209.
10. Maududi, "Fallacy," 215. Note how Maududi, like Qutb, presents conflicting statements on rationalism.
11. Maududi, "Fallacy," 210. Maududi holds Westerners also to this peculiar display of loyalty. He explains, for example, that a British citizen should not be expected to criticize British law (Maududi, "Fallacy," 210). He believes that any criticism of one's source of law, whether by British lawmakers or Muslims, indicates a treasonous lack of faith.
12. Maududi, "Fallacy," 210, 217.
13. Maududi, "Fallacy," 210, 218, 219, 217.
14. Maududi, "Fallacy," 211, 210.
15. Maududi, "The Political Theory of Islam," in Moaddel and Talattof, *Contemporary Debates*, 271.
16. Compare to Soroush's distinction between an "Islam of Identity" and an "Islam of Truth." Soroush describes the former as "a guise for cultural identity and a response to what is considered the 'crisis' of identity" (Soroush, "Intellectual Autobiography," in *Reason, Freedom, and Democracy,* 23).
17. Qutb, *Social Justice,* 12, 167; Qutb, "Jihad," in Moaddel and Talattof, *Contemporary Debates,* 234, 243.
18. Qutb, *Social Justice,* 168. The poll tax in actuality did not provide the level of equality that Qutb claims. The tax ostensibly was levied in exchange for military protection by the Muslim army; however, the non-Muslims who paid the poll tax were not given the option of joining the army instead of paying the tax. Moreover, the Qur'anic verse (9:29) about the poll tax abrogates "(*nasakha*) the hundreds of other verses on the subject of the treatment of the Other revealed prior to them" (Sohail Hashmi, "The Qur'an and Tolerance: An Interpretive Essay on Verse 5:48," *Journal of Human Rights* 2, no. 1 [March 2003]: 83). The verses that appear prior to 9:29 distinguish with less aggression Jews and Christians from Muslims.
19. Qutb, "Jihad," 224, 225. Note that here Qutb uses *jihad* to describe the struggle for Islam by means of the sword as well as through intellectual and emotional persuasion. Qutb, whom many consider a militant Islamist, believes that *jihad* has multiple meanings rather than simply and singly "holy war."

20. Qutb, *Social Justice,* 93, 94; Qutb, "Jihad," 243.
21. Qutb, *Social Justice,* 12. Qutb here refers, of course, to the miracles found in the Hebrew and Christian scriptures.
22. This contradicts Qutb's epistemology, which emphasizes divine command over rationality.
23. Qutb, *Social Justice,* 12.
24. Qutb, "Islam as the Foundation," in Moaddel and Talattof, *Contemporary Debates,* 201. Qutb's epistemology resonates strongly with discourse theories foundational to postcolonial studies. Literary criticism, found in the writings of Derrida, Saussure, Foucault, and Macherey, questions the assumed innocence of language in social and economic institutions. The human subject and language relate to each other in complex ways. Although humans create language, language also constructs the human subject. To borrow from Althusser, one might say that the production and dissemination of colonialist language constitute Ideological State Apparatuses. The media, schools, newspapers, journals, and books reinforce the ideology that ensures compliance among the colonized. Qutb does not believe, however, that the power of colonialist discourse is totalizing in its disempowerment. He grasps the insidious power of language in perpetuating colonialism and recommends that the carriers of colonialist language, such as books and humanistic writings, be eliminated. He believes that colonized Egyptians will be able to move beyond colonialism once these epistemological barriers are removed. See Derrida, *Writing and Difference*; Foucault, *History of Sexuality*; Macherey, *Theory of Literary Production*; Saussure, *Course in General Linguistics.*
25. Qutb appears to make an exception for some works of Western literature, which he claims may offer insight into the essential spirit of Islam. Prior to his life as a religious scholar, Qutb was a literary critic and poet. (Indeed, at this time he would have been introduced to the French philosophical schools that produced Camus and Sartre, both of whom influenced postcolonial thinkers such as Fanon.) His affection for literature, even if it comes from the West, appears to have lingered. Qutb's belief that some works of literature, regardless of their origin, carry universal messages is mirrored by his adaptation of Western philosophy to critique and move beyond colonialism.
26. Qutb, "Islam as the Foundation," 206, 203. Fanon explains the politicized view of technology and science in colonies. In his *Dying Colonialism,* Fanon examines the seemingly incomprehensible rejection and then use of inoculations and the radio by the Algerian population. The Algerians initially rejected the radio because they saw no use for purchasing expensive equipment when it broadcast French news relevant only to French occupiers. Algerians likewise avoided inoculations because they viewed physicians who administered them as part of the larger colonialist regime. When Algerians began to resist colonization, however, they viewed the radio and inoculations as beneficial to their cause. They established their own radio station, The Voice of Fighting Algeria, which gave a reason for native Algerians to invest in radios. Algerians also began to train their own medical staff to administer inoculations and provide other medical services in order to keep their civilian and fighting populations healthy. See Childs and Williams, *Post-Colonial Theory,* 53.
27. Qutb, "Islam as the Foundation," 200.
28. Qutb, "Islam as the Foundation," 204. He cites 2:109, 2:120, and 3:100, as well as *hadith* from Hafiz Abu Yali on the authority of Hazrat Hammand

and Shaabi. Qutb does not indicate to the reader that he has quoted selectively and out of context. Although the Qur'an does warn Muslims that Jews and Christians will attempt to proselytize them, the Qur'an also states (in a passage immediately following one quoted by Qutb) that "they are not all alike; some of the People of the Book are a nation upstanding, that recite God's signs in the watches of the night, bowing themselves, believing in God and in the Last Day, bidding honour and forbidding dishonour, vying one with the other in good works; these are of the righteous" (3:110) (A. J. Arberry, *The Koran Interpreted* [New York: Touchstone, 1955], 88).

29. Soroush, "Tolerance and Governance," in *Reason, Freedom, and Democracy,"* 138. See also 'Abdolkarim Soroush, "Dr. Soroush's Interview with Seraj" (April 1997), www.drsoroush.com/Interviews_E.htm.
30. Soroush, "Autobiography," 25. Also see Soroush, "Idea of a Democratic Religious Government," in *Reason, Freedom, and Democracy,"* 128; Soroush, "Life and Virtue," in *Reason, Freedom, and Democracy,* 30.
31. Soroush, "Tolerance and Governance," 139.
32. Soroush, "Tolerance and Governance," 139.
33. Soroush, "Doctrine and Justification," in *Reason, Freedom, and Democracy*, 72.
34. Soroush, "Doctrine and Justification," 72.
35. Soroush, "Tolerance and Governance," 138, 144–45, 150. With regard to the various channels that provide checks on excesses of power, economist Amartya Sen argues similarly that in the contemporary age, tangible results of a democratic government are strongly tied to the presence of a free press. A free press, Sen reasons, manages the corruption and excesses in government that, when left unchecked, eventually deprive its citizens of basic human rights.
36. Soroush, "Tolerance and Governance," 150.
37. Soroush, "Autobiography," 21. Soroush previously refers to problems of the global economy, modernity, and information technology, which leaders of the Islamic revolution had not considered realistically.
38. The idea that the texts of the colonizers can be co-opted and used by the colonized as a form of resistance is explored by Bhabha in his ideas on hybridity and mimicry. Tools used by colonizers to control the ideology of the colonized, found especially in the transmittal of languages and literature, can be used as a form of resistance because discourse has a power independent of those who claim to "own" it. Ranging from taunting to full-scale violent rebellion, methods of resistance are often adaptations of colonial strategies. Bhabha modifies Said's critique of Orientalism and explains how "colonial discourse is never wholly in the control of the colonizer" (Childs and Williams, *Post-Colonial Theory,* 136). The idea of political and economic revolution, from French history and found in Marxist theory, was successfully adopted by the Iranians to overthrow a colonial puppet regime.
39. Soroush, "Autobiography," 23; Soroush, "Tolerance and Governance," 151.
40. Soroush, "Life and Virtue," 49–53; Soroush, "Let Us Learn from History," in *Reason, Freedom, and Democracy,* 184–89.
41. Maududi, "Fallacy," 215; Qutb, *Social Justice,* 94.
42. Mary Ann Glendon, *A World Made New: Eleanor Roosevelt and the Universal Declaration of Human Rights* (New York: Random House, 2001), 100.

43. Abid Ullah Jan states that the "supposed problem of Islamic 'intolerance' is in fact principled resistance demonstrated by the Muslims who stand up for justice even against their own self-interests" (Jan, "The Limits of Tolerance," in Abou El Fadl, *Place of Tolerance,* 45). Jan argues that "Islam is still uncommonly tolerant of other peoples and religions" and notes the disparity in judgments on Islam and other religions (Jan, "Limits," 45). He asks, "Why doesn't anyone talk about the crisis of tolerance in Judaism when dozens of Palestinians have been killed on a weekly basis for the last thirty-five years? Why is the media silent about intolerant Hinduism that has relentlessly oppressed Kashmiri Muslims for the last fifty-five years? Why didn't the analysts speculate about intolerance in Christianity when 300,000 Muslims were butchered in Bosnia? And why not now, as Muslims face the wrath of Russians in Chechnya? Why are the lectures on tolerance directed at Islam alone? Simply because the victim of September 11 was the United States" (Jan, "Limits," 45–46). Although Jan does make excellent points about the lack of focus on religions other than Islam, he fails to support fully his claim that the identity of the victim solely determines these judgments about religion. Certainly, attacks on the most powerful nation will result in massive media attention to all aspects of the event, including the religious identity of the assailants, but there are reasons other than the religious identity of the victim that lead to an enormous amount of attention focused on the event itself, the victims, and Islam. With regard to September 11, not only was the attack targeted toward a country in peacetime, but also it was staged without warning and aimed at civilians. The sheer number of civilians killed and the method of attack were also highly unusual. Finally, the perpetrators of the events of September 11 identified their act as performed in the name of Islam. They themselves proclaimed Islam as the religious motivation for and source of their actions.
44. Maududi, *Islamic Movement,* 101–2.
45. Qutb, "Islam as the Foundation," 201.
46. For example, eugenics, the study of "good breeding" made infamous by Nazi Germany, but studied throughout Europe and the United States, was considered a hard science well into the twentieth century. Articles on eugenics were published in the top science and medical journals, and prominent research universities sponsored eugenics studies and experiments. One might also consider the relationship between the aeronautical sciences and the cold war. The progress of the United States and former Soviet Union in the 1950s and 1960s in this field was undoubtedly influenced by the need for each country to prove its greatness through a symbolic mission to the moon. Medical research is also tightly bound to the health needs of the country in which it takes place. In wealthier countries, for instance, research efforts are often poured into tertiary care concerns, rather than the primary care needs that are the focus of researchers in poorer countries. Although many, like Qutb, claim that the hard sciences are objective, all research is designed and managed by humans in specific historical, social, political, and economic contexts that define and limit their project. See Gadamer, *Truth and Method.* Gadamer asserts that the "being-in-itself toward which research, whether in physics or biology, is directed, is *relative to the way being is posited in its manner of* inquiry. . . . Each science, as a science, has in advance projected a field of objects such that to know them is to govern them" (Gadamer, *Truth and Method,* 452, italics added).

47. Soroush, "Life and Virtue," 49–53; Soroush, "Let Us Learn from History," 184–89.
48. Edward Said illustrates Habermas's theory in his classic *Orientalism,* wherein he demonstrates how literature and scholarship produced by European "Occidental" scholars enabled colonial domination of the "Orient."
49. The "optimism" that pervades the theories of Gadamer and Soroush could indicate a rather high view of human nature, whereas the pessimism and caution seen in the stances of Maududi, Qutb, and Habermas seem to reflect the experience of human suffering, domination, and cruelty. Whereas a high anthropology seems naïve, an unwavering low view of human nature prevents us from attempting to extricate others and ourselves from deplorable situations. These low views of human nature, however, must contain within them some possibility for progress. If there is no point in emerging from the quagmire, why bother? Said and Althusser have been criticized for presenting such a monolithic view of the colonial machine that there remains little hope for resistance or rebellion. Yet, colonized peoples resisted and rebelled and were able to win their independence. Colonialism and other regimes of repression are complex and within these regimes sources of resistance have been found. Said, in *Culture and Imperialism,* critiques his own work in *Orientalism* and states that "it was the case nearly everywhere in the non-European world that the coming of the white man brought forth some sort of resistance. What I left out of *Orientalism* was that response to Western dominance which culminated in the great movement of decolonization all across the Third World. . . . Never was it the case that the imperial encounter pitted an active Western intruder against a supine or inert non-Western native; there was *always* some form of active resistance, and in the overwhelming majority of cases the resistance finally won out" (*Culture and Imperialism* [New York: Vintage Books, 1993], xii; see also Childs and Williams, *Post-Colonial Theory,* 108; Loomba, *Colonialism,* 33). Sources of resistance were to be found not only within the local culture but also within the colonizing culture. The diversity within seemingly monolithic cultures contributed to the eventual overthrow of colonial governments.

## CONCLUSION

1. Maududi and Qutb appear to have read and been influenced by each other's works. Soroush, who is of a younger generation, did not engage in scholarly dialogue with Maududi and Qutb, but is able to read their works and comment upon them. The dialogue that takes place within Islam is not only one that happens synchronically, that is across geography and within the same historical epoch, but also one that needs to happen diachronically, that is, through history. Being able to read a text in the present moment and to examine it as a historical document that reflects the concerns of its time offers the scholar the opportunity to straddle two worlds at once. True, the author of the historical text (or any text, for that matter) does not actively engage the reader, but does exert an influence into a future time when the text is read. Diachronic dialogue is not the same as synchronic dialogue, but it is nonetheless significant in the influence it wields. In synchronic dialogue, the participants in discussion have the advantage of responding instantaneously to questions and of clarifying points that appear misunder-

stood. This kind of response is not possible in reading historical texts, but historical texts do make an appearance in future dialogues and are used to question, respond, and clarify.

2. See Soroush, "Tolerance and Governance," in *Reason, Freedom, and Democracy*," 133, 135, 142.
3. See Maududi, *Let Us Be Muslims*, 100.
4. Gadamer, *Truth and Method*, 383–89.
5. See Seyla Benhabib, *Situating the Self: Gender, Community, and Postmodernism in Contemporary Ethics* (New York: Routledge, 1992), 54–55.
6. Martin Marty, David Guinn, and Larry Greenfield, *Religion and Public Discourse* (Park Ridge, IL: Park Ridge Center, 1998), 4.
7. Kathryn Tanner, "Public Theology and the Character of Public Debate," *Society of Christian Ethics: The Annual* (1996): 85.
8. Ronald Thiemann, *Religion in Public Life: A Dilemma for Democracy* (Washington, DC: Georgetown University Press, 1996), 136.

# GLOSSARY OF FOREIGN WORDS AND PHRASES

| | |
|---|---|
| *ahl al-kitab* | People of the Book, typically Jews and Christians, referring to believers whose divine scripture testifies to the same Abrahamic God; may be extended to believers of other religious traditions. |
| *'aql* | Rationality or reason used to determine Islamic law. |
| Ash'ari | Tenth- to twelfth-century Sunni legal school that emphasized the primacy of divine revelation over human reason in determining morality. |
| *bay'ah* | Literally, the clasping of hands; oath of loyalty taken by electors to caliph. |
| *dhimmis* | Protected status given typically to People of the Book who lived under Muslim rule; they were allowed to continue their religious beliefs and practices in exchange for payment of a special tax. |
| *hadith* | Record of the teachings and practices of Muhammad. |
| *hajj* | Pilgrimage to Mecca; one of the five pillars of Islam. |
| *hidaya* | Divine spark to provide moral guidance to humans. |
| *ijma* | In Islamic jurisprudence, the consensus of legal scholars. |
| *ijtihad* | In Islamic jurisprudence, innovative or independent legal interpretation achieved through intellectual and religious struggle; shares the same root as "jihad." |
| *imamah* | Divinely chosen leadership of the Muslim community. |
| *ismah* | Divinely inspired intellectual and emotional virtue found in prophets and imams. |
| *jahiliyyah* | The period before Muhammad's revelation characterized by ignorance of the monotheistic nature of God. |
| *jihad* | Literally, struggle; refers both to outward struggles to defend Islam and to inner struggles of personal will. |
| *khilalfa* | Representation of God's will on earth by humans. |

| | |
|---|---|
| *madhi* | Eschatological ruler who will restore faith in Islam and justice in the world at the end of time. |
| madrasa | School for the study of Islamic law and sciences; generalized term for any Muslim school. |
| *majlis* | Iranian parliament. |
| *maslahat* | In Islamic jurisprudence, rulings made in the public interest. |
| Mut'azilte | Eighth-century theological movement that held the necessity for both reason and revelation in determining morality. |
| *salaf* | First three generations of Muslims; considered exemplars of Islamic belief and practice. |
| *Salafiyyah* | Reform movement of the early twentieth century to purify and restore Islam to its idealized formative era. |
| *salat* | Prayer; one of the five pillars of Islam. |
| *satyagraha* | Sanskrit for the "force of truth"; the principle that guided Mahatma Gandhi's nonviolent campaign for Indian independence. |
| *sawm* | Fasting; during Ramadan, fasting is considered one of the five pillars of Islam. |
| *shahada* | Personal witnessing of God; the first of the five pillars of Islam. |
| *'shar* | Revelation of divine law. |
| *shari'a* | Islamic law based on the Qur'an, *sunna*, and *hadith*. |
| *shura* | Collaboration or consultation among Muslims to decide public affairs. |
| *sunna* | Traditions and practices of Muhammad. |
| *taqwa* | Pious belief and conduct based on a consciousness of God. |
| *tawhid* | Unity of God that permeates all aspects of humanity and the created world. |
| ulama | Muslim clergy or religious scholars. |
| *umma* | Muslim community. |
| Wahhabism | Eighteenth-century social and political movement incorporated into Saudi rule that emphasized the unity of God, opposed saint veneration, and idealized the formative era of Islam. |
| *wilayah* | Custodianship or rule over Muslims by a divinely chosen ruler. |
| *zakat* | Charity or almsgiving intended to purify one's wealth; one of the five pillars of Islam. |

# BIBLIOGRAPHY

Abou El Fadl, Khaled. "Islam and the Challenge of Democracy." *Boston Review*, April/May 2003.

———. *The Place of Tolerance in Islam*. Edited by Joshua Cohen and Ian Lague. Boston: Beacon Press, 2002.

Abu Rabi', Ibrahim. *Intellectual Origins of Islamic Resurgence in the Modern Arab World.* Albany: State University of New York Press, 1996.

Abu Zayd, Nasr. *Rethinking the Qur'an: Towards a Humanistic Hermeneutics.* Utrecht, Netherlands: Humanistics University Press, 2004.

Afkhami, Mahnaz, ed. *Faith and Freedom: Women's Human Rights in the Muslim World.* Syracuse, NY: Syracuse University Press, 1995.

Ali, 'Abdullah Yusuf. *The Holy Qur'an: Text and Translation.* Lahore, Pakistan: Muhammad Ashraf, 1938.

Althusser, Louis. *Lenin and Philosophy*. London: New Left Books, 1971.

An-Na'im, Abdullahi Ahmed, ed. *Human Rights in Cross-Cultural Perspectives: Quest for Consensus.* Philadelphia: University of Pennsylvania Press, 1992.

———. *Toward an Islamic Reformation: Civil Liberties, Human Rights, and International Law*. Syracuse, NY: Syracuse University Press, 1990.

Arberry, A. J. *The Koran Interpreted.* New York: Touchstone, 1955.

Arjomand, Said. *Turban for the Crown: The Islamic Revolution in Iran*. New York: Oxford University Press, 1990.

Arkoun, Mohammad. *L'islam morale et politique* [Moral and Political Islam]. Paris: Desclée de Brouwer, 1986.

al-'Ashmawy, Muhammad. *Against Islamic Extremism.* Edited by Carolyn Fluehr-Lobban. Gainesville: University Press of Florida, 1998.

Audi, Robert, and Nicholas Wolterstorff. *Religion in the Public Square.* Lanham, MD: Rowman and Littlefield, 1997.

Bauer, Joanne R., and Daniel A. Bell, eds. *The East Asian Challenge for Human Rights.* Cambridge: Cambridge University Press, 1999.

Beitz, Charles. "Human Rights as Common Concern." *American Political Science Review* 95, no. 2 (June 2001): 269–82.

Benhabib, Seyla. *Situating the Self: Gender, Community, and Postmodernism in Contemporary Ethics.* New York: Routledge, 1992.

Berman, Paul. "The Philosopher of Islamic Terror." *New York Times Magazine*, March 23, 2003.

Bhabha, Homi. *The Location of Culture*. New York: Routledge, 1994.

———. “Of Mimicry and Man: The Ambivalence of Colonial Discourse.” *October* 28 (1984): 125–33.

Bielefeldt, Heiner. “Muslim Voices in the Human Rights Debate.” *Human Rights Quarterly* 17, no. 4 (1995): 587–617.

Cannon, Katie. *Black Womanist Ethics*. Atlanta: Scholars Press, 1988.

Cèsaire, Aimè. *Discourse on Colonialism*. Translated by Joan Pinkham. New York: Monthly Review Press, 2000.

Childs, Peter, and R. J. Patrick Williams. *An Introduction to Post-Colonial Theory*. New York: Prentice Hall, 1997.

Cleveland, William. *A History of the Modern Middle East*. 3rd ed. Boulder, CO: Westview Press, 2004.

Dahl, Robert. *On Democracy*. New Haven, CT: Yale University Press, 1998.

Dalacoura, Katerina. *Islam, Liberalism and Human Rights: Implications for International Relations*. London: I. B. Tauris, 1998.

Daniel, Elton. *The History of Iran*. Westport, CT: Greenwood Press, 2000.

Derrida, Jacques. *Writing and Difference*. Chicago: University of Chicago Press, 1980.

Donnelly, Jack. “Human Rights and Human Dignity: An Analytic Critique of Non-Western Conceptions of Human Rights.” *American Political Science Review* 76, no. 2 (June 1982): 303–16.

———. *Universal Human Rights in Theory and Practice*. Ithaca, NY: Cornell University Press, 1989.

Elster, Jon. *An Introduction to Karl Marx*. New York: Cambridge University Press, 1990.

Enayat, Hamid. *Modern Islamic Political Thought*. Austin: University of Texas Press, 1982.

Engineer, Ashgar Ali. *Islam and Liberation Theology: Essays on Liberative Elements in Islam*. New Delhi, India: Sterling, 1990.

Esposito, John, and John Voll. *Islam and Democracy*. New York: Oxford University Press, 1996.

———, eds. *Makers of Contemporary Islam*. New York: Oxford University Press, 2001.

Euben, Roxanne. *Enemy in the Mirror: Islamic Fundamentalism and the Limits of Modern Rationalism: A Work of Comparative Political Theory*. Princeton, NJ: Princeton University Press, 1999.

Fakhry, Majid. *Ethical Theories in Islam*. Leiden, Netherlands: E. J. Brill, 1991.

Fanon Frantz. *Black Skins, White Masks*. New York: Grove Press, 1968.

———. *A Dying Colonialism*. New York: Grove Press, 1965.

———. *The Wretched of the Earth*. Translated by Constance Farrington. New York: Grove Press, 1963.

Fasching, Darrel, and Dell deChant. *Comparative Religious Ethics: A Narrative Approach*. Malden, MA: Blackwell, 2001.

Foucault, Michel. *The History of Sexuality: An Introduction*. New York: Vintage, 1990.

Gadamer, Hans-Georg. “Reflections on My Philosophical Journey.” In *The Philosophy of Hans-Georg Gadamer*, edited by Lewis Edwin Hahn, 3–63. Peru, IL: Open Court Publishing, 1997.

———. *Truth and Method.* 2nd rev. ed. Translated by Joel Weinsheimer and Donald G. Marshall. New York: Crossroad, 1991.

Geertz, Clifford. *The Interpretation of Cultures.* New York: Basic Books, 1973.

Glendon, Mary Ann. *A World Made New: Eleanor Roosevelt and the Universal Declaration of Human Rights.* New York: Random House, 2001.

Goldziher, Ignaz. *Introduction to Islamic Theology and Law.* Translated by Andras Hamori and Ruth Hamori. Princeton, NJ: Princeton University Press, 1981.

Gramsci, Antonio. *A Gramsci Reader: Selected Writings, 1916–1935.* London: Lawrence and Wishart, 2000.

Gutierrez, Gustavo. *A Theology of Liberation.* Maryknoll, NY: Orbis Books, 1988.

Habermas, Jürgen. "On Systematically Distorted Communication," *Inquiry* 13, no. 3 (Autumn 1970): 205–18.

———. *The Theory of Communicative Action.* Vol. 1, *Reason and the Rationalization of Society.* Translated by Thomas McCarthy. Boston: Beacon Press, 1984.

———. "'Wahrheitstheorien,' Wirklichkeit und Reflexion" [Theories of Truth: Reality and Reflexion]. In *Festschrift für W. Schulz,* edited by H. Fahrenbach, 211–65. Pfüllingen, Germany: Neske, 1973.

Hallaq, Wael. *A History of Islamic Legal Theories: An Introduction to Sunni usul al-fiqh.* New York: Cambridge University Press, 1997.

Harrison, Beverly. *Making the Connections: Essays in Feminist Social Ethics.* Boston: Beacon Press, 1985.

Hashmi, Sohail. "The Qur'an and Tolerance: An Interpretive Essay on Verse 5:48." *Journal of Human Rights* 2, no. 1 (March 2003): 81–103.

Held, David. *Models of Democracy.* Stanford, CA: Stanford University Press, 1996.

Hodgson, Marshall G. S. *The Venture of Islam.* Vol. 1, *The Classical Age of Islam.* Chicago: University of Chicago Press, 1975.

———. *The Venture of Islam.* Vol. 3, *The Gunpowder Empires and Modern Times.* Chicago: University of Chicago Press, 1977.

Hourani, Albert. *A History of the Arab Peoples.* Cambridge, MA: Belknap Press of Harvard University Press, 1991.

Hourani, George. *Reason and Tradition in Islamic Ethics.* Cambridge: Cambridge University Press, 1985.

Ignatieff, Michael. *Human Rights as Politics and Idolatry.* Princeton, NJ: Princeton University Press, 2001.

Ishay, Micheline, ed. *The Human Rights Reader.* New York: Routledge, 1997.

Jackson, Sherman. *On the Boundaries of Theological Tolerance in Islam: Abu Hamid al-Ghazali's Faysal al-Tafriqa.* New York: Oxford University Press, 2002.

Juergensmeyer, Mark. *Terror in the Mind of God: The Global Rise of Religious Violence.* Berkeley and Los Angeles: University of California Press, 2000.

Keddie, Nikki. *An Islamic Response to Imperialism: Political and Religious Writings of Sayyid Jamal al-Din al-Afghani.* Berkeley and Los Angeles: University of California Press, 1983.

———. "Is There a Middle East?" *International Journal of Middle East Studies* 4, no. 3 (July 1973): 255–71.

Kerr, Malcolm. *Islamic Reform: The Political and Legal Theories of Muhammad Abduh and Rashid Rida*. Berkeley and Los Angeles: University of California Press, 1966.

King, Richard. *Orientalism and Religion: Postcolonial Theory, India, and the "Mystic East."* New York: Routledge, 1999.

Kurzman, Charles, ed. *Liberal Islam: A Sourcebook*. New York: Oxford University Press, 1998.

Lawrence, Bruce B. *Defenders of God: The Fundamentalist Revolt against the Modern Age*. Columbia: University of South Carolina Press, 1989.

Lijphart, Arend. *Patterns of Democracy: Government Forms and Performance in Thirty-Six Countries*. New Haven, CT: Yale University Press, 1999.

Little, David, John Kelsay, and Abdulaziz Sachedina. *Human Rights and the Conflict of Cultures: Western and Islamic Perspectives on Religious Liberty*. Columbia: University of South Carolina Press, 1988.

Little, David, and Sumner B. Twiss. *Comparative Religious Ethics*. San Francisco: Harper and Row, 1978.

Loomba, Ania. *Colonialism/Postcolonialism*. New York: Routledge, 1998.

Macherey, Pierre. *A Theory of Literary Production*. Boston: Routledge and Kegan Paul, 1978.

Majid, Anouar. *Unveiling Traditions: Postcolonial Islam in a Polycentric World*. Durham, NC: Duke University Press, 2000.

Marshall, Christopher. *Crowned with Glory and Honor: Human Rights in the Biblical Tradition*. Scottsdale, PA: Herald Press, 2002.

Marsot, Al-Sayyid. *A Short History of Modern Egypt*. New York: Cambridge University Press, 1985.

Marty, Martin, David Guinn, and Larry Greenfield. *Religion and Public Discourse*. Park Ridge, IL: Park Ridge Center, 1998.

Maududi, Abul A'la. *Human Rights in Islam*. Lahore, Pakistan: Islamic Publications, 1977.

———. *The Islamic Law and Constitution*. Translated by Khurshid Ahmad. Lahore, Pakistan: Islamic Publications, 1960.

———. *The Islamic Movement: Dynamics of Values, Power, and Change*. Edited by Khurram Murad. Leicester, UK: Islamic Foundation, 1984.

———. *Let Us Be Muslims*. Edited by Khurram Murad. Leicester, UK: Islamic Foundation, 1985.

———. *Selected Speeches and Writings of Maulana Maududi*. Karachi, Pakistan: International Islamic Publishers, 1981.

Mayer, Ann Elizabeth. *Islam and Human Rights: Tradition and Politics*. Boulder, CO: Westview Press, 1991.

McCarthy, Thomas. *The Critical Theory of Jürgen Habermas*. Cambridge: Polity Press, 1984.

Mernissi, Fatima. *The Veil and the Male Elite: A Feminist Interpretation of Women's Rights in Islam*. Translated by Mary Jo Lakeland. Reading, MA: Addison-Wesley, 1991.

Mitchell, Timothy, *Colonizing Egypt*. Berkeley and Los Angeles: University of California Press, 1991.

Moaddel, Mansoor, and Kamran Talattof, eds. *Contemporary Debates in Islam: An Anthology of Modernist and Fundamentalist Thought*. New York: St. Martin's Press, 2000.

Mottahedeh, Roy. *Mantle of the Prophet: Religion and Politics in Iran*. New York: Simon and Schuster, 1985.

Mueller-Vollmer, Kurt. *The Hermeneutics Reader*. New York: Continuum, 1994.

Nasr, Sayyed. *The Vanguard of the Islamic Revolution: The Jama'at-i Islami of Pakistan*. Berkeley and Los Angeles: University of California Press, 1994.

Nussbaum, Martha. *Women and Human Development: The Capabilities Approach*. New York: Cambridge University Press, 2000.

Thomas Pogge, "How Should Human Rights Be Conceived?" In *The Philosophy of Human Rights,* edited by Patrick Hayden, 187–210. St. Paul, MN: Paragon, 2001.

Palmer, Richard. *Hermeneutics*. Evanston, IL: Northwestern University Press, 1969.

Perry, Michael. *The Idea of Human Rights: Four Inquiries*. New York: Oxford University Press, 1998.

Qutb, Sayyid. *In the Shade of the Qur'an*. Vols. 1–18. Translated by M. A. Salahi and A. A. Shamis. Leicester, UK: Islamic Foundation, 1999–. Not all volumes have been translated.

———. *Milestones*. Translated by S. Badrul Hasan. Karachi, Pakistan : International Islamic Publishers, 1981.

———. *Social Justice in Islam*. Translated by John B. Hardie. New York: Octagon Books, 1970.

Rahman, Fazlur. *Islam and Modernity*. Chicago: University of Chicago Press, 1982.

———. "Law and Ethics in Islam." In *Ethics in Islam: Ninth Giorgio Levi Della Vida Biennial Conference*, edited by Richard G. Hovannisian, 3–15. Malibu, CA: Undeila Publications, 1985.

———. *Major Themes of the Qur'an*. Minneapolis: Bibliotheca Islamica, 1989.

Rawls, John. *The Law of Peoples*. Cambridge, MA: Harvard University Press, 1999.

———. *Political Liberalism*. New York: Columbia University Press, 1996.

Sachedina, Abdulaziz. *The Islamic Roots of Democratic Pluralism*. New York: Oxford University Press, 2001.

Safi, Omid, ed. *Progressive Muslims: On Justice, Gender, and Pluralism*. Oxford: Oneworld Publications, 2003.

Said, Edward. *Culture and Imperialism*. New York: Vintage Books, 1993.

———. *Orientalism*. New York: Vintage, 1978.

Saussure, Ferdinand. *Course in General Linguistics*. Chicago: Open Court Publishing, 1988.

Schaefer, Brian. "Human Rights: Problems with the Foundationless Approach." *Social Theory and Practice* 31, no. 1 (January 2005): 27–50.

Sen, Amartya. "Democracy as a Universal Value." *Journal of Democracy* 10, no. 3 (1999): 3–17.

———. "Elements of a Theory of Human Rights." *Philosophy and Public Affairs* 32, no. 4 (Fall 2004): 315–56.

———. "Human Rights and Asian Values." In *Ethics and International Affairs*, edited by Joel Rosenthal, 170–93. Washington, DC: Georgetown University Press, 1999.

Shapiro, Susan. "Rhetoric as Ideology and Critique: The Gadamer-Habermas Debate Reinvented." *Journal of the American Academy of Religion* 62, no. 1 (1994): 123–50.

Shklar, Judith. "The Liberalism of Fear." In *Political Thought and Political Thinkers*, edited by Stanley Hoffman, 3–21. Chicago: University of Chicago Press, 1998.

Shue, Henry. *Basic Rights: Subsistence, Affluence, and U.S. Foreign Policy.* Princeton, NJ: Princeton University Press, 1980.

Singh, Jyotsna. *Colonial Narratives/Cultural Dialogues: "Discoveries" of India in the Language of Colonialism.* New York: Routledge, 1996.

Soroush, 'Abdolkarim. "Dr. Soroush's Interview with Seraj." April 1997. www.drsoroush.com/Interviews_E.htm.

———. "The Evolution and Devolution of Religious Knowledge." In *Liberal Islam: A Sourcebook*, edited by Charles Kurzman, 244–51. New York: Oxford University Press, 1998.

———. *Reason, Freedom, and Democracy in Islam: Essential Writings of 'Abdolkarim Soroush.* New York: Oxford University Press, 2000.

Soyinka, Wole. *Death and the King's Horseman.* New York: Hill and Wang, 1975.

Tamimi, Azzam. *Rachid Ghannouchi: A Democrat within Islamism.* New York: Oxford University Press, 2000.

Tanner, Kathryn. "Public Theology and the Character of Public Debate." *Society of Christian Ethics: The Annual* (1996): 79–101.

Taylor, Charles. *Philosophy and the Human Sciences.* New York: Cambridge University Press, 1985.

Thiemann, Ronald. *Religion in Public Life: A Dilemma for Democracy.* Washington, DC: Georgetown University Press, 1996.

Twiss, Sumner B., and Bruce Grelle, eds. *Explorations in Global Ethics: Comparative Religious Ethics and Interreligious Dialogue.* Boulder, CO: Westview Press, 2000.

Wadud, Amina. *Qur'an and Woman: Rereading the Sacred Text from a Woman's Perspective.* New York: Oxford University Press, 1999.

Waltz, Susan. "Universal Human Rights: The Contribution of Muslim States." *Human Rights Quarterly* 26, no. 4 (2004): 799–844.

Walzer, Michael. *On Toleration.* New Haven, CT: Yale University Press, 1997.

Wehr, Hans. *A Dictionary of Modern Written Arabic.* 3rd ed. Edited by J. Milton Cowan. Beirut: Librairie du Liban, 1980.

Yearly, Lee. *Mencius and Aquinas: Theories of Virtue and Conceptions of Courage.* Albany: State University of New York Press, 1990.

# INDEX